THE ADVENTURES OF

ROBIN HOOD

Retold by Mark Taylor

Contents

CHAPTER 1

The Invitation

"**W**ell, what is this? Kindling for this evening's fire?"

The pile of sticks on Robin's lap clattered to the floor as he jumped up from his bench to face the booming voice.

"Father! You startled me!" He stooped to pick up one of the sticks. "You know what I'm making, sir. Arrows! Look at how straight and strong they are."

"Hmmm." Master Hugh Fitzooth frowned as he inspected Robin's work. "Good, perhaps," he said. "But not good enough."

"Hugh! Don't be so hard on the lad!" Robin's mother had entered the back of the house to greet her husband. "Come here and relax. Take off your shoes and give me your bow. It's time for dinner, and we have some important news."

At last the man smiled, as she embraced him around the waist and pecked him on the cheek.

"News!" He raised one eyebrow. "What kind of news has traveled all the way to this simple house deep in the forest?"

"The most exciting news possible," Robin said, and he held up a scroll. "Here, read this."

Fitzooth glanced at his wife. "It's from my brother," she said. He pulled away from her as he took the scroll. "He's invited Robin to come see the Nottingham fair."

Robin opened his mouth to speak again, but the man's frown had returned, and Robin's mother looked worried.

Fitzooth carried the scroll to the brighter light at the open door. "So George Montfichet of Gamewell wants to show Robin something that he can't find here—is that it?"

"Hugh," the woman protested. "He invited us all to visit him. I know he's a Norman and you're a Saxon." She had her arm around his waist again, and her fingers touched his cheek. "But he is an open, honest man. Why couldn't we visit him? You need a break from the drudgery of this forest!"

Fitzooth squinted at the scroll. "Aah, the Normans write with such foolish flourishes," he muttered. "Read it to me later," he said as he thrust the parchment at his wife. "Now it's time to eat!"

Robin was trimming the wicks and lighting the candles at the homemade table where they would eat their meal. His father smiled at him and mussed his hair as he took his place. Robin sat across from him as his mother spread the meal before them.

"I've been making arrows all afternoon," Robin said. "I have almost two dozen. What do you think?"

"In time, Robin, in time," the man said, ignoring the stack of sticks that Robin had piled on the table between them. "Surely, all this activity has made you hungry, hasn't it?" He eagerly cut into the meat pie his wife had set before him. She and Robin fell silent as they, too, ate the one-dish meal.

After several bites, Fitzooth began examining the arrows one-by-one.

"Crooked," he said of one, and tossed it into the coals smoldering in the fireplace behind him.

"Too short," he said of the next, and pitched it into the fire as well.

"The point is not sharp enough," he described another.

Robin said nothing, but his cheeks were pink.

"Well, now, this one will shoot," his father said and laid the arrow at the end of the table. And so it went throughout the meal. By the time the last bite was finished, only five good arrows remained.

"Hugh…," his wife began quietly.

"Aah, the boy is a good bowman," Fitzooth interrupted. "He knows it, and so do I." He smiled again. "But who will ever help him be his best if I don't?"

Neither Robin nor his mother said a word. And then Fitzooth's eye fell on the scroll across the room where his wife had laid it.

"Your brother!" he roared. "Is that it? Do you suppose your brother, at one fancy fair in

Nottingham, will do what a lifetime in this forest couldn't accomplish?"

"No, no, no!" For the first time, Robin's mother raised her voice. "Honestly, Hugh, be reasonable! It is a simple invitation, that's all!"

"May I read you the letter?" Robin asked. And for the first time all evening, his father looked at his son—really looked at him, and noticed the beard appearing beneath his warm cheeks. His face was lean and strong. The muscles in his arms bulged beneath his deerskin shirt. This was no boy asking his father for permission to play in the woods. Robin was almost a man.

Suddenly Hugh Fitzooth grew very quiet himself. "Yes," he said. "Yes… of course. Read it. Read me the letter, Robin."

Robin unrolled the scroll and took on an official-sounding voice.

"From George Montfichet, of the Hall at Gamewell, near Nottingham, Squire of all Sherwood Forest," he read, "with greetings and a prayer for God's blessing on his sister Eleanor and on her husband, Master Hugh Fitzooth, Ranger of the King's Forest at Locksley. Happiness be with you all.

"I send this with the desire that tomorrow, June fifth, both of you will ride to me at Gamewell and bring with you your fine son Robin. The Fair at Nottingham will happen for three days this week, and we expect it to be a marvelous event.

"I know Robin will enjoy it, and I most deeply desire that you will bring him with you here."

Robin paused and looked up at his mother. She smiled and nodded at him.

"And that's not all," he continued reading. But he seemed to fidget, and his voice was not as strong as before. "I would like Robin to stay with me for awhile, perhaps as long as a year. I am a lonely man, for now I have no son of my own. I will treat Robin as if he were that son, and return him to you in June next year.

"This I send by the hand of Warrenton, my man-at-arms. Written by my hand at Gamewell, the fourth day of June, in the year of our Lord one thousand one hundred and eighty-eight.

"(Signed) Montfichet."

Robin rolled the scroll in his hands and waited for his father to respond. The man stood and walked toward an open window to see the sun's setting rays filter through the trees surrounding their house.

"Please, Father," Robin finally broke the silence. "Say that we may all go tomorrow. You have often promised me that you would take me to the fair."

"I cannot leave the forest," Fitzooth replied quickly. "The woods are full of robbers. I must oversee the foresters and guarantee that no deer are killed and stolen. It is my duty to the King himself!"

Fitzooth saw Robin's disappointment and hurried on. "But you may go with your mother," he said, "if Friar Tuck will go with you too. I will ride with you tomorrow as far as his house, and send two servants to accompany you the rest of the way."

Eleanor Fitzooth joined her husband at the window. "Are you sure you won't come with us?" she asked. "My brother's man, Warrenton, frightened me with his talk of outlaw bands."

"Ah, he only wanted to be sure I'd refuse your brother's invitation! If the Sheriff of Nottingham is doing his job at all, then your journey will be safe."

He turned toward Robin. "Go, get your clothes ready. Take all your pack will hold, for you will be there for a year. Learn all about the proper life in the city. But don't forget your bow."

He put his hand on Robin's shoulder. "Remember always to depend on your own hands and your own eyes—nothing else will ever serve you as well. If Warrenton can show you how to fashion arrows within the year, I'll ask no more of brother George of Gamewell."

"You shall be proud of me, sir. I swear it. But I will be home within the month. My mother needs my help here."

Robin climbed the ladder to his loft. Fitzooth returned to his window and saw the darkening dusk outside. "Men shall talk of you, my son," he whispered to the trees. "And, if God is good, I may live to hear them."

CHAPTER 2

The Robbers

R obin was awake long before dawn, and by the time the sun sparkled on the dewy grass, he was already dressed. His jacket and leggings were as green as the leaves of the forest.

Soon, but not soon enough for Robin, the two servants had saddled the horses, and they were ready to travel. But not until they loaded a mule with all the baggage his mother had decided she needed for her visit.

Robin was pacing outside the house, stringing and unstringing his bow. Finally, he called toward the door. "If we don't leave soon, we might as well eat our lunch here!"

"We're coming, we're coming," his mother said, lifting her gown above the dirt as she hurried outside.

Robin's father helped his wife onto her small white horse. "A bit anxious to be leaving Locksley, my son?"

They aimed their horses down the path away from the house. Two servants led the mule ahead of them. Robin rode between his mother and father.

"I love my home," Robin answered. "And I love both of you. But I can't wait to see the fair! Don't worry, I'll be back in a month."

"No, a year, Robin. A year! I insist on it."

Within an hour they were at Copmanhurst, the sleepy crossroads where a sole priest lived in a small stone building beside ruins of the chapel. His two sad-eyed hounds bayed and barked and howled as Robin and his family rode close.

The monk came to his door and peered over a fence that surrounded his two-room house.

"Good morning, Father." Robin was the first to greet the man. "Tie your dogs and get your horse—we're going to the Nottingham fair, and you're coming with us!"

The monk shook his head slowly. "I may not leave my post here for such trivial pursuits," he said, looking at the ground.

"Oh please ride with my wife and my son," Fitzooth interrupted. "George of Gamewell has sent for Robin, but I cannot go with him there. I need you to teach him and guide him while he's away from home."

"I have a marvelous veal pie for our lunch," Eleanor added. "And a loaf of fresh bread and a flask of wine."

Friar Tuck's eyes brightened. But his tone remained solemn. "Do not think you can tempt me with worldly pleasures," he said. "If the King's ranger bids me on a journey, then I will obey him. Duty demands it! But nothing else could move me from my service here."

He disappeared inside and returned soon with a thin cloth satchel. No one could deny that his life was simple, but anyone could also see that he had not lived on roots and water alone. He bent his round body to chatter with his dogs, huffing and puffing through red cheeks as he worked to tie them.

Meanwhile, Hugh said good-bye to his family. "Protect your mother," he told Robin. "Take these arrows that I have made myself, and learn how to make more that are just as good. You have a steady hand and a strong eye. Improve your skills, and I will give you control of some part of the forest when you return."

He embraced his son and kissed his wife and then guided his horse back toward home. They watched until he stopped to turn and wave farewell with his cap. Then he disappeared into the green of the trees.

The little party rode slowly toward Nottingham. Robin had talked non-stop from Locksley to Copmanhurst. But now he was

strangely silent. He felt a sadness he had not expected and did not understand.

Squirrels skittered above them, and rabbits scurried before them. Puddles of sunshine lighted the winding path under arching branches of giant maples and oaks.

It was almost noon when they came to a spot completely shaded by the thick leaves.

Just ahead, Robin caught sight of a stag, with ears twitching beneath antlers that spread at least four feet wide. Robin reached for his bow, and he remembered the new arrows his father had given him. "All of the deer in the forest belong to the King, don't they, Father?"

"Every beast within Sherwood belongs to our King, lad," Friar Tuck answered.

"Do you think I could knick that stag, Father?"

The monk looked at Robin's mother. "Let's take a rest in these cool shadows," he said to her. "Isn't it time for us to enjoy that hearty

20

meal you've prepared? I'm tired, and besides," he added with lowered voice and a slight smile, "I think the boy needs something to take his attention."

"I don't want to stop in this darkness," she said. "Robin, ride close to me. Your uncle's man Warrenton told me yesterday—"

But then her voice was drowned by the shrill sound of a bugle coming from the forest. At once they were surrounded by six ragged rascals.

"Toll, toll," cried the sandy-haired leader with a cocky grin. His cohorts had seized the servants before they could draw their daggers or find their bows. "Pay your toll, and then you can continue."

"Who are you?" Robin demanded. "And why should we pay you anything?"

Just then the man saw the deer that Robin had been watching. Quickly he fitted an arrow to his bow and sent it flying toward the beast bounding away from them.

"Aah, what kind of aim was that?" said Robin. He also shot at the stag. But by now it had almost disappeared, and Robin's arrow fell far short.

"And what kind of aim was THAT?" the leader said, and all six of the hooligans roared with laughter.

"Enough of this!" Robin shouted, his eyes flashing. "Out of the way, or we'll whip you all!"

But the leader only smiled. "First, please pay your toll," he said, his hands on his hips and his legs spread wide. By now the servants were bound on the ground. The priest looked pale as he gripped his horse's reins, and Eleanor Fitzooth sat stiffly on her horse. Tears filled her wide eyes.

"How dare you demand toll of a woman!" Robin shouted.

"Everyone who goes here must buy their freedom," the leader said calmly, "—both man and woman. Pay now, and when you return, you shall pass unharmed."

"Take my mule," Robin offered.

"It isn't enough," the leader answered.

"Here, take my purse, then," Robin's mother said, reaching into her pack. "There's little enough in it, for we are a poor family." Her voice was thin and tight.

Robin raised his arm to stop her. "Ask a toll of the church," he said to the leader. "The church is rich, and later the priest will grant forgiveness to all of you."

The robbers laughed again. "We have no quarrel with God," one of them shouted from the path.

"And we have no quarrel with you!" Robin answered.

"Then quit quarreling!" the leader said. He wasn't smiling now. "Pay your toll, and let's be done with it. We have others to visit in Sherwood Forest."

"Let me shoot with you for the freedom of the forest," Robin offered. "If I win, we can pass with no toll. If I lose, you may have all but my mother's horse. She will ride to Gamewell, and I'll be your hostage until she returns."

"With a hundred crowns in each hand, then," the leader replied.

"It's a deal," Robin said. "The monk will be our judge. Now, Father Tuck, choose our target ... and pray for Heaven to speed my arrows toward the mark."

The frightened Friar could hardly speak, but he managed to point to a white-barked tree about fifty yards ahead of them. "The knot on the side of the birch," he squeaked.

"A great choice, Father," the chief robber said. He turned to Robin, who had already fit his arrow to his bow. "You go first."

Robin clinched his teeth, concentrated on the target, and pulled the bow tight. He let the arrow fly, and it sailed straight, twanging into the knot on the side of the birch.

"Nice," said the robber simply. "But your arrow has hit the edge of the mark." His arrow sang through the summer air, landing with a thud beside Robin's, directly in the center of the knot.

The priest, who still seemed pale, glanced at Robin and back at the robber. "You have

won the first round," he told him. His eyes
searched for the next target, but then he heard
leaves rustling, twigs breaking, and horse's
hooves pounding in the woods behind them.

Suddenly, from three directions, more than
forty of the King's Foresters thundered from
the forest.

"Seize them!" cried the lead rider. "It's Will-
o-the-Green and his men!"

But just as quickly, the six robbers had van-
ished into the thicket.

Robin spun around. "Who are these men?"
he asked his mother.

"They have been sent by the Sheriff of
Nottingham," she answered between deep
breaths. "Your father told us the Sheriff was
guarding these woods."

"Madam, please tell us what happened."
The lead rider had stopped and was now helping Eleanor from her horse. She tried to
answer, between interruptions from the servants.

"They came out of nowhere," said the first.

"We could do nothing to defend ourselves," said the second.

The captain of the foresters, Master John Ford, introduced himself to Eleanor. He tried to calm the servants as his men, in twos and threes, searched the woods for the wily robbers.

Friar Tuck persuaded Eleanor to open her meal. And she offered a portion to Captain Ford, who gladly joined them.

"What name did you shout before?" Robin wanted to know more about the impudent band that had almost ruined their journey.

"Will-o-the-Green," replied Ford. "King Henry himself has outlawed the rascal. He killed his brother, although many say it was an accident. They say he was loyal before the King banished him," he added with a sneer. "They say he kills the King's deer only for his own survival. I say he is a bandit who should be hung!"

After more than thirty minutes the foresters returned with nothing, not even a sight of the six renegades.

"They are a crafty lot," Ford said. "We think they have underground hideouts, with secret entrances and hidden passages." He volunteered to accompany Eleanor and her family the rest of the way to Gamewell. Once again Robin rode silently, deep in thought.

What would Father have done if he had been with us? he wondered. *Would Will-o-the-Green have been so bold with him?*

Someday I'll shoot with Master Will again, Robin vowed to himself. *Someday I'll show him that I'm the better marksman!*

He brooded through the rest of their journey. But Robin could have never guessed how soon his dream would come true.

CHAPTER 3

The Welcome

Dusk had darkened the woods by the time they arrived at Gamewell. The castle loomed before them, lights shining through every window in the heavy walls.

Captain Ford blew his bugle as the entourage approached the sparkling moat, and soon the creaking bridge was lowered to let them in.

Master Montfichet—George of Gamewell as the people called him—was inside, waiting to greet them. The Squire was an elderly man. His bright eyes were surrounded by deep wrinkles above sunken cheeks, and white hair curled from under his little round cap. He wore long black robes that hung loose on him, like those a monk would wear. As Robin and his mother climbed down from their horses, the Squire stepped forward to greet them.

"You have come!" he said. "I am delighted. Nell," the Squire said to his sister. "You can't imagine how glad I am to see you." He kissed her on both cheeks, and Robin remembered that he had never heard anyone else use this nickname with his mother. It sounded strange to him.

A half-dozen servants busied themselves with the party's baggage and animals while the Squire heard the captain's report. He listened quietly, with a half frown, and warmly thanked the officer for his help.

Soon several maids had whisked away the Squire's sister. Montfichet had kindly ushered the priest to quarters close to his own, and now he was alone with Robin.

"I hope you'll be happy with the arrangements we've made for you," said the Squire. And Robin had no doubt, from the man's manner and from all he'd already seen, that he would be happy indeed.

Soon the Squire opened a door and said, "This will be your chamber." Robin's eyes fell first on the wide, white bed, covered with more brightly colored clothes than Robin had ever before seen in one place. "They're for you," said the Squire. "You'll have a new outfit for the fair—you have several to pick from."

A high latticed window looked out on the courtyard two stories below. A bench sat in one corner. It was crowded with a hodgepodge of items: unused, rolled parchments; a feather pen in an inkwell; several bottles of colored, scented water; and a wooden tray holding a gold chain.

Two walls were decorated with floor-to-ceiling tapestries. One showed a mighty

deer leaping through the forest. Two knights on galloping horses jousted on the other tapestry.

The low ceiling was raftered with polished beams. Behind the door was a gleaming sword, suspended by a leather belt.

"Wear it to dinner this evening," said the Squire with a smile. "We will eat in an hour," he added, and then he was gone. Robin was left alone.

It didn't take Robin long to prepare for dinner. He was hungry, and he was anxious to visit with his host. Soon he appeared at the castle's great hall, where a thousand flickering candles invited him to enter. The Master of Gamewell greeted him, and his mother smiled with approval from her place at the magnificent table.

Robin sauntered toward her. His jacket was royal blue. His gold chain reflected candlelight, and the handsome sword rode securely on his hip.

35

"I will build you a castle like this one day," he said, taking her hand. "Tell me, sir," he said to the Squire, "how much must I earn to afford so excellent a dwelling?"

Montfichet laughed heartily. "The King himself gave me this castle many years ago," he said. "It was a reward for valor in a battle I fought for him."

"Then I shall also fight for the King," Robin vowed. "For my family, too, deserves so fine a place."

"I will teach you—you can count on that," the Squire replied. "Just be sure you're fighting for the right King," he added, his face more serious now. "King Henry's son, Prince John, gathers his knights and threatens the throne. Do not lend your strength to such rebellion. But vow that your allegiance shall always be to the King God has put over us."

Yes, Robin thought, *loyal to the King, and united against the likes of Will-o-the-Green.* And as he enjoyed his uncle's lavish feast,

Robin felt sure that he would someday know true greatness.

CHAPTER 4

The Riot

The Nottingham Fair had never been more colorful—or more full of merchants and merriment.

Bright pennants—yellow, red, or green— waved from the top of every tent. The murmuring, moving crowd below them pressed against each other—some buying, some selling, and even more who simply walked and watched it all.

Boys played mandolins or flutes while girls sang ballads and hoped for a donation. Women spread fresh-baked treats on trays, and their husbands hollered above the crowd, offering the sweets for sale.

Acrobats entertained in open patches of grass. Jugglers kept balls or berries circling in the air. And fortune tellers invited those passing by to enter their tents.

Robin hurried from amusement to amusement, trying to take it all in. But one band of entertainers interested him the most.

The players, three sons and their father, were from Cumberland. Robin learned that they made their living traveling throughout the country, from fair to fair. As their father blew furiously into a wooden flute, the boys sang songs, told riddles, turned cartwheels, and did magic.

Between tricks they would wrestle with each other—and then challenge the young men in the crowd to wrestle them for a prize.

It seemed that no one ever earned the prize. The three were agile and fast, and Robin never saw them lose. But Robin was sure he could beat one of them, especially the youngest, smallest brother.

"Do you think I should try?" Robin asked his uncle.

"No!" the Squire said. "Your mother is waiting for us, Robin. We must be going!" He waved to the three men-at-arms he had brought with him, and together they walked away. But after taking only a few steps, Montfichet stopped and looked back at the players.

"Since you're so interested in sport, I have an idea," the Squire said to Robin, and he was back in front of the wrestlers in two long strides.

"Young men," he said with authority. "I have a proposition. I will give a purse of silver pennies to the one who wins your next wrestling match—two out of three falls."

The father of the troupe took up the challenge at once. "Come one, come all," he shouted to the gathering crowd. "Which fine Nottingham youth will win against these seasoned wrestlers from Cumberland?"

Young men jostled in a circle around them. Soon a thin-faced fellow stepped to the center of the crowd. The circle widened to make room for the wrestling, while even more of the fair goers crowded around the outside to see what happened. Robin and Montfichet found themselves surrounded by several dozen sweaty, swearing roughnecks who taunted the wrestlers and laid wagers on who would win.

The two youths had stripped off their shirts and grabbed hold of each other's shoulders. They pulled and tugged and strained. The Nottingham challenger was thin but well muscled, a surprising match for the thick-limbed Cumberland professional.

The Cumberland boy tried to trip the challenger, but instead he almost fell himself.

"You'll need to do better than that!" came a quip from the back. It was a voice Robin had heard before. At once he turned and caught a glimpse of the sandy-haired robber from Sherwood. It was Will-o-the-Green! The robber smiled at him, the same cocky grin he had displayed on the path in the forest. "Don't give up, Nottingham!" Will hollered at the wrestler again. And then he was gone.

Robin tried to get through the riffraff to the renegade. He pushed and pulled, just as the wrestlers grabbed and tugged. Finally he fought his way out of the mob, only to hear a groan come up from the men. The Nottingham youth had been pinned twice, and in

short order. Robin stood panting outside the circle, looking first this way and then that. But Will-o-the-Green was nowhere to be seen.

"Spend the money worthily, as you have won it," the Squire said to the red-faced Cumberland winner, and he handed him the purse.

As the crowd dispersed, the Squire looked for Robin.

"Sir, I must tell you about Will-o-the-Green, the robber from Sherwood."

"What about him?" Montfichet asked.

"I saw him. I saw him here—watching the wrestlers!"

"That's impossible," Montfichet replied.

"No, I know I saw him," Robin said again. "How could I forget such a rascal?"

"Well, where is he now?"

"He got away," Robin answered.

"Then we'll tell the Sheriff," said the Squire. "How impudent of that upstart to act as if he were an upstanding citizen!"

By now they had reached Robin's mother. "And what do you think of the fair?" she asked with a pleasant smile.

He had just begun to tell her about the wrestlers and Will-o-the-Green, when they heard a roar behind them. They turned to see a mob of ruffians—maybe a hundred of them—running right toward them! The troupe of four players led the crowd, racing for their life.

"Get back! Be careful," the Squire ordered his sister, and she cowered under the canopy of the booth where they'd met. He blew a silver whistle hanging from his belt, and his three men-at-arms came running.

"Hel-l-l-l-p us!" the father of the three wrestlers cried when they spied the Squire. Montfichet stood firmly in the path, watching them run toward him. They scurried behind him to face the rest of the crowd.

"Halt, there!" the Squire demanded. He held up his hand, and amazingly, they obeyed the white-haired, wrinkled man. "What in Heaven's name is happening here?" he demanded.

The youngest wrestler, still out of breath, answered first. "They came after us with sticks and clubs," he stammered.

"Who?" asked the Squire.

"The Nottingham youth who lost the wrestling match—and his friends. They demanded a rematch, but we told them no. And so they tried to grab the purse."

"How ashamed you Nottingham men should be!" said Montfichet. "This Cumberland lad won fair and square. Is this how you treat guests to your city?"

"Easy for you to say, old man," the Nottingham wrestler sneered at him. "I am the one he tricked. I am the one he cheated. I am the one who deserves—"

"Be quiet, now!" Montfichet roared. "Break up this crowd, or we'll have you all arrested."

"We'll see about that," shouted one of the throng, and he raised his stick toward Montfichet. His man-at-arms stopped the blow, but not before the other guards were already battling the young toughs.

Robin and the little tumbler forced Montfichet and his sister away from the fighting crowd and into the tent behind the booth. Then, together they jumped on the back of the Nottingham wrestler who tried to follow them.

They rolled around and around in the dirt, hitting and hollering. Meanwhile, the throng had melted into a churning lump of punching fists and kicking legs.

Robin and his cohort lay on top of their captive. "What should we do now?" Robin said, gasping for breath.

"Hold him!" the wrestler answered, a thin trickle of blood coming from his nose.

Just then they heard strong, firm voices above the mayhem.

"Break it up now! Stop the fighting!"

"The Sheriff's men!" Robin whispered.

A dozen of them waded into the crowd, pulling fighters apart and hitting others with their short, fat sticks. As soon as the people saw them, they began to run away.

"Let me go," the Nottingham captive whimpered.

"Go far, then," Robin sneered as he freed him. He ran with the others, through the fair and into the maze of city streets beyond. None of them wanted to face the Sheriff's prison or chains.

Robin and the wrestler stood and slapped the dirt from their jackets and legs.

"I should tell you my name," the wrestler said. "I am Will Stutely."

"And I am Robin Fitzooth."

"Shall we be friends?" asked Will.

"Of course," said Robin. "If you had not helped me, my mother and my uncle would have been run over by that mob."

"And if you had not helped us, we might have been killed!"

"Is it over?" The feeble voice came from the tent behind them. Robin and Will looked at each other and stifled a laugh.

"Uncle! Mother! Come out. It's safe now."

Robin's mother poked her head between the canvas flaps. "Robin, help me," she said with a quivering voice. "Your uncle is sick!"

CHAPTER 5

The Fugitive

Robin and Will threw open the canvas tent flaps and discovered the pale Squire sprawled on the ground inside.

"What's wrong?" Robin asked.

"He feels faint," Robin's mother answered.

"I'm fine," the Squire gasped. "Really." He raised himself on a trembling elbow. "Just help me, and we'll be out of here."

Robin and Will took his arms and slowly lifted him to his feet.

"That's fine, that's fine," he said. "We'll go to the Sheriff's castle. We must report this to him." He turned to the wrestlers and their father. "Come with us to the Sheriff," he said. "He must hear your story, and we should all wait there till we know there'll be no more trouble."

Slowly they walked the half-mile to the castle. Only the Squire rode, while one of his men led the horse. "He complained of pains in his chest," Eleanor told Robin. But she swore him to secrecy. "He doesn't want anyone to know."

The Sheriff himself greeted them inside his castle. Robin watched curiously as the chubby, overdressed man fussed and fretted over the Squire.

"Honorable Sir, my whole castle is at your disposal," the Sheriff babbled. "We will catch the upstarts who did this, of that I assure you! Nottingham shall not be the kind of place where this kind of lawbreaking goes unpunished. And you can tell King Henry that yourself!"

Robin suspected that the Sheriff was far more concerned about his reputation with the King than he was worried about the Squire's health. But whatever the motive, the Sheriff treated Montfichet and his whole party as honored guests.

Robin's mother was attended by the Sheriff's daughter and her maids. Montfichet's men-at-arms found refreshments in the pantry, along with Will's brothers and father. But Robin persuaded his uncle to allow Will to stay with him as his own servant. And the Squire was too weak to argue.

Robin and Will accompanied Montfichet to one of the Sheriff's chambers, where the Squire rested, still pale and still short of breath.

"Tomorrow we must return to Gamewell," he said sadly. "All of this is too much for me."

"It doesn't matter. I've seen enough of the fair," Robin answered.

"You'll return on the day after tomorrow for the tournament. I'll not let you miss that. Young Will here can be your servant. And I'll send my own man Warrenton with you as well."

"We'll talk about that then," Robin soothed him. "For now you must rest."

The Squire slept well that night—after enjoying a lavish feast with his family at the Sheriff's banquet table. And he spent the next day resting, too, in his own quarters at Gamewell.

Warrenton himself toured the castle and its grounds with Robin and Will. Will's father had gladly left him in Robin's service. "There's a future for you with him," he had told his son. And now Will seemed as eager as Robin to discover all of Gamewell castle's secrets.

Warrenton was the perfect guide. He knew the corridors and corners of this dwelling as well as anyone. And even though he came close to boring Robin and Will with his stories about each tapestry or carving, the two were fascinated with the place. They hung on every description of secret treasure. And they hooted and cheered when he showed them each new hidden hallway or concealed door.

Soon they were outside. Robin had never walked through orchards or gardens more beautiful or better cared for. And then he saw

the targets lined against a row of pines at the edge of a smooth, green lawn.

"Who is the archer here?" he asked.

"The master himself," Warrenton answered. "Despite his age, he's one of the finest marksmen in Nottingham—and you're looking at the one who taught him!"

"Really!" said Robin. "Do you have a bow and quiver here?"

"Crossbow and longbow and arrows a-plenty," Warrenton said with a smile. "And all that Gamewell has I am to give you—the master ordered it! Now send young Will to that hut beside the targets, and he can fetch whatever you wish."

Robin raised one eyebrow toward Will, and he ran to do the errand. Robin and Warrenton walked after him. They had come within a yard of the small building when they heard a scuffle inside, followed by a stifled shout.

"Warrenton! Something's in there! What could it be?"

"I—I don't know!" Warrenton's eyes were wide. "I've never seen an animal on this lawn." He reached for a small knife fastened to his belt, when, just then, Will stumbled out of the hut, held at the mouth by a young man wielding a dagger.

"Warrenton!" the man with the weapon called, in a desperate whisper. "Warrenton, tell these idiots to be quiet!"

"Geoffrey," the servant said. "It is Squire Montfichet's own son, Geoffrey! My lord, what are you doing here?"

"Who are these loudmouths?" Geoffrey ignored Warrenton's question.

Warrenton had gained his composure. "This is your cousin, Sir," he said, pointing to Robin. "And you are threatening his servant!"

"So," the young Montfichet sneered, "my cousin Robin has come to claim my place at the castle." He shoved the trembling Will at Robin, wide-eyed and limp. "Don't worry. There's nothing here I would trade for my

life of freedom. Take it all! I have far more important battles to fight elsewhere on this island."

"Geoffrey—I—I've been here only a day." Robin's head was reeling. "I—I didn't know whether you were alive or dead. There's been no time to ask your father."

"Relax," Geoffrey replied. "Whatever happens here will be alright with me." He paused and sized up his younger cousin. *More of a man than I would have imagined,* he thought. *He reminds me of myself a few years ago—eager and ignorant.*

The young Montfichet stepped toward Robin and embraced him. "It's good to see you, Robin." His face was tan and lean. His beard was bushy and untrimmed. His clothes were dark and worn.

"It's good to see *you*," Robin replied, still confused. "But why are you hiding here?"

Geoffrey stiffened and pointed his dagger at Robin's chin. "You must tell no one you have seen me!" His tone was again defiant. "No one! I am an outlaw here—"

"But surely your father would help—"

"You don't know what you're saying," Geoffrey interrupted. "Just make sure you check that wagging tongue of yours! Do you understand?"

"Uh—of course," Robin stammered.

"Now, Warrenton," Geoffrey turned to the servant. "You must help me. I need a horse and armor and a lance. I intend to ride at Nottingham in the joustings."

"Whatever you say, sir, but—"

"Don't worry. I'll be disguised. And I'll never lift my visor." He smiled bitterly. "A hungry wolf in my father's domain."

"I'll do my best," said Warrenton. "But how will I find you?"

"This will be my hiding place," said Geoffrey, and he backed into the doorway of the hut. "Bring the horse and arms to me at midnight."

"I'll help you," Robin said.

Geoffrey cocked his head and considered the offer. "I believe I can trust you," he answered. "Robin, see that the trappings and armor are made of good steel. I want them decorated with red leather—the sheath and lance as well. You will know me at the jousts, then, when you see the red."

"I will not miss the jousts," Robin said. "And you can count on me." He looked at Warrenton. "You can count on us."

"At midnight, then," Geoffrey repeated, and he extended his right hand to Robin. Their handshake was firm.

Just then they heard voices coming from the garden that bordered the walk beyond the lawn behind them. "Back into the hut, now!" Warrenton whispered.

"Is my father well?" Geoffrey asked from inside the doorway.

"Well enough," Robin answered, "although at Nottingham yesterday—"

"Yes, I heard."

"You heard?"

"It doesn't matter how." Geoffrey was completely inside the hut now. The voices from the garden grew louder. "Tell me that you will always protect him as valiantly as you did yesterday."

"Robin!" Warrenton pulled at his jacket. "We must go!"

"You have my word," said Robin.

Geoffrey shut the door and bolted it as Robin, Warrenton, and Will turned back toward the castle.

"Will," said Robin, "you must not breathe a word of this to anyone."

"Breathe a word about what?" Will raised his brows over wide eyes. "I don't even know what you're talking about!" Robin smiled.

"And so you see, Robin," Warrenton said aloud, so that his voice would carry across the lawn. "There is a fine art to arrow-making, an art I have perfected over my lifetime."

Their eyes caught sight of Friar Tuck strolling toward the walk with Captain John Ford of the King's Foresters. Their talk was spirited—they had not seen the three, or Geoffrey. But Ford looked up when he heard Warrenton's voice.

"Well, see who's here, Father," he said to his companion. Robin and the others smiled and walked to meet them. "Does the Squire's man try to teach you about arrows?" the forester asked. "If you want to know about arrows, like Will-o-the-Green's, then listen to me. Each of his is almost one yard long, and winged with the feathers of an eagle."

"Peacock," corrected the priest. "Let me show you, Master Ford. I found this one in the forest after you had rescued us from him."

Friar Tuck put his hand on Robin's shoulder and directed him toward the castle. "But enough of this," he said. "The Master Montfichet has sent me to find you. He wants to speak with you, Robin. And if you're smart you'll listen carefully to everything he says. Listen carefully and answer slowly. His ideas are not to be taken lightly."

But even he has no idea of what we've seen and heard here today! thought Robin. "Yes, Father, whatever you say," he answered. "I will listen…. I will listen."

CHAPTER 6

The Getaway

Robin leaned against the cold stone wall in the corridor outside the Squire's chambers. His stomach was doing flip-flops.

The Squire had asked him to become his son! To take the Montfichet name, and to inherit everything at Gamewell! Robin's mind spun with the possibilities—and the problems!

"But what about Geoffrey?" Robin had protested.

"Geoffrey is no longer my son," the Squire had said grimly.

"But, Master, why?"

The Squire's answer did not satisfy him. Oh, it was true that Geoffrey was an outlaw. He had joined the rebellion of Prince John, King Henry's son, against the King's throne. The King had condemned Geoffrey to death, but Montfichet had begged for mercy. The King reduced Geoffrey's sentence to life imprisonment. But just as Montfichet was journeying home from his audience with the King, Geoffrey fled for Scotland.

"Not only is he a criminal, he is ungrateful and disrespectful!" the Squire had raged to Robin. "He has shamed me before the whole land, and before the King himself!"

Robin remembered his cousin hiding on the castle grounds this very moment. His mind was filled with the memory of his tan face, his brave words, his firm handshake. Robin would not betray him, not now, not ever. He knocked on his mother's door and found her inside, looking pale and worried.

"You've talked to the Squire," she said.

"Yes, and he told me he had talked with you.... Mother, I will not steal Geoffrey's inheritance!"

"You are not stealing it. My brother is giving it to you!"

"Then you think I should say yes?"

She turned away from him and wrung her hands. "I don't know what I think," she cried. "My brother is a good man—"

"And my father? My father is a good man too!"

"Of course he is, Robin. He would only want what is best for you. Didn't he insist that you stay here for a year?"

"Mother, I will not answer the Squire without first talking with Father."

"But what if the Squire won't wait?"

"What choice does he have?" Robin asked her. He had taken her hands in his. Robin needed time. Time to think. Time to see if somehow his uncle and his cousin could get together. Time to hear his father's opinion.

"We won't worry about this till tomorrow," he told his mother, wiping a single tear from her cheek.

"You're right," she agreed. She was calmer as he left her. But Robin was still upset. *Why had Geoffrey returned to Gamewell? And why was he riding in the tournament tomorrow?* He wanted to see him again, but he knew he dared not return to the hiding place before dark.

But Warrenton insisted that he be the one to meet Geoffrey at midnight.

"Why you?" Robin demanded. They talked in noisy whispers in the courtyard, away from the servants preparing the evening meal.

"Because no one questions what I do or where I go," Warrenton answered. "What will a guard think if he catches you wandering around the castle in the middle of the night?"

Robin couldn't argue with that. But later, after another generous meal at the Squire's table, Robin caught Will and told him his plan.

They agreed they would sneak to the hut hiding place as soon as everyone was asleep and the castle was quiet.

The air was chilly and the night was still when Robin and Will climbed out of the window in Robin's room. The courtyard below them reflected the eerie glow of a full moon. Robin went first, finding a firm foothold in the ivy on the castle wall.

They tiptoed through the courtyard and the gardens. Instead of crossing the lawn, they crept around the edge, trying to stay in the shadows. The archery targets were silvery sentinels, guarding the hut where they had left Geoffrey.

Robin reached it first. He gently tapped the door, which he expected to be bolted. But, instead, it pushed open with his touch.

"There's no one here!" he whispered to Will, once they were both inside.

"Do you suppose—oh!" Robin heard Will tumble.

"Will! What happened!"

"There's a hole," Will answered, out of breath. The voice came from below Robin. "There's a hole in the—" And then Robin fell in too! He landed right on top of Will, knocking him down again.

"Are you alright?" Robin said to Will, as he tried to regain his footing. The air felt damp and cold. The walls seemed close to them, but they couldn't see a thing. A shaft of moonlight entered the door of the hut six feet above them, but in this hole everything was black.

"We've got to get out of here," Will said.

"Here, I'll give you a boost," Robin said. "See if you can reach the floor of the hut."

Just then they heard the snapping of twigs overhead.

Robin grabbed Will's arm. "Sh-h-h! Someone's outside."

They stood frozen, as the yellow glow of a lantern cast bouncing shadows into the hut

73

above them. They tried to back away from the hole, whose shape they could begin to see now. But then they saw the candle-lit figure of a face they knew. It was Warrenton!

He lowered his lantern to the hole in the floor of the hut. But he jumped back, frightened, when he saw the two men below.

"Warrenton!" Robin said. "Get us out of here!"

"Oh—it's—it's you," Warrenton stammered. He lowered his arm and lifted first Will, then Robin, out of the hole. "What are you doing here?" he demanded. He had regained his composure and assumed a take-charge attitude.

But Robin was not intimidated. "What are *you* doing here?" he said, with equal force.

"You knew I was to meet Master Geoffrey at midnight," Warrenton answered.

"Where is Geoffrey?" Robin asked.

"You've missed him."

"But we didn't see him. How did he get away?"

"Through the hole," Warrenton answered. And he lowered his lantern through the floor of the hut again. The chamber below them was a full six feet wide, and Robin could see now that it was not a room, but a tunnel.

"It's a secret passage," Warrenton explained. "There are many of them around here. It leads to the Sherwood forest. Geoffrey is hiding there tonight with the outlaws in the woods. I delivered his horse and lance to him there."

"So why did you come back to the hut?" Robin still wasn't sure he should trust Warrenton.

"I stopped here to make sure it was secure," Warrenton answered. He peered out the door of the hut, across the moonlit lawn. "We must get back to the castle before we're discovered," he said.

"You must not tell anyone about any of this," Warrenton said to Robin and Will as they sneaked back to the castle. "Geoffrey's life is at stake!" They slipped through the garden gate, and his whisper became quieter and more urgent. "No one saw you leave, did they?"

"No one," Robin assured him. They entered a back servants' door.

"Now off to your room," Warrenton said. For the first time he smiled, and he put his arm on Robin's shoulder. "Tomorrow is the tournament, and you have no idea what's in store for you there."

Robin shook the man's hand. "Thank you, Warrenton," he said, and he began to believe that Warrenton wanted only what was best for Geoffrey—and for him.

He and Will tiptoed through shadowy corridors—alone and unseen, except by one pair of eyes. The curious Friar, unable to sleep, had heard them clambering down the courtyard walls. And now he waited, with his door ajar, to see them creep back to their rooms.

CHAPTER 7

The Contest

Robin awoke late the next morning. In bed the night before, he had stared at moonlit rafters for an hour before slipping into a fitful sleep. He had expected excitement at Gamewell. But this was far more than adventure.

The events of the last two days turned over and over in his mind as he nibbled at a breakfast of bread and berries in one corner of the kitchen. He was staring at the wall, with a crust in one hand, when Warrenton burst into the room.

"There you are!" he said. Robin looked up, surprised. "The tournament is this afternoon."

"Of course, I know that."

"But you aren't ready!"

"Ready for what?"

"For the archery contest!"

"I knew about the jousts," Robin answered. "I knew nothing of an archery contest."

"There's much that you don't know," Warrenton said with a chuckle. "That is why I am to teach you! Master Montfichet has instructed me to share my shooting secrets with you."

Robin still didn't move.

"Well, what are you waiting for?" Warrenton demanded. "We haven't much time. You need to practice."

They returned to the same archery targets they had seen yesterday. But today Warrenton already had bows and a quiver full of arrows ready for Robin to use. The feel of the bow in his hands, the twang of the arrows, and the advice of Warrenton soon made Robin forget anything else except the thrill of shooting.

He listened as Warrenton told him how to alter his aim, how to stand for each shot, and how a breeze might affect his arrow's path. Even Warrenton was impressed with Robin's ability. In less than an hour, he had mastered every pointer Warrenton offered.

It was shortly after noon when Warrenton, Will, Captain Ford, and Robin began the hour-long ride to Nottingham. Soon Robin again became distracted by his thoughts of Geoffrey and the Squire, and he realized he was lagging behind the others. He heard the babble of a brook beside the path, and the sound of the water made him thirsty.

He tied his horse to a tree and looked for the stream. It was shallow and muddy by the road, but Robin could hear its rushing from farther into the woods. He followed the sound till he came to a spot where the stream ran clear and deep.

He was on his stomach, lapping the water with his hands, when he heard voices beyond him. He stayed low and listened as he tried to see who was coming.

There were two men, both dressed poorly, in muslin shirts with tattered leggings. "I say we should nab him," said the first. He was taller, with a dirty gray beard. "Our friend Will doesn't know what he's doing, tying up with some nobleman. There's no future in it, Tom."

"I don't care about Will. All I care about is the bounty on his head. I tell ya, Andrew, it would do me good to get the King's ransom in *my* pocket!"

"Aye, but they say the Scarlet Knight is a shrewd one—and a strong one too. Do you think we could ever catch him? And if we did, would Will let us take him in?"

"If we found him in the woods, killed by some hunter's arrow, we'd be stupid not to trade the body for the reward, now, wouldn't we?" He jabbed his friend in the arm, and they both laughed loudly.

Robin's blood ran cold. Here he'd found two more of his cousin's enemies. It seemed he was not safe with royalty, not safe at home, and not safe with the outlaws of the forest, either! Robin had heard enough. He needed to get away.

The bandits kept walking slowly, unaware of Robin. He crawled along the forest floor toward his horse.

"What was that?" said one of the outlaws as Robin's knees and hands broke sticks beneath him. He stopped, silent.

"Ah, it was just a squirrel," the shorter one said. "You're sure gettin' jumpy in your old age!"

They laughed again as Robin caught sight of his horse. He stood to run for it. In a flash he was flying down the road on her back. He felt the whiz of an arrow past his ear, and he lowered his head to the horse's neck. Soon another arrow flew by. And then a sharp stinging jolted his right shoulder. He'd been hit!

He slapped the animal's sides with both feet, and she galloped even faster. Ahead of him he saw his three companions. And ahead of them loomed the gates of Nottingham. He sped past them into the city, and pulled his horse to a stop.

"Robin!" Will called after him. Robin started to dismount, but his rubber-band legs wouldn't hold him. "Robin!" He heard Will's voice again, just before the sky began to spin and everything turned black.

"Robin!" He heard the voice again, but this time from the end of a long tunnel. "Robin, are you alright?" The voice was coming closer now. Robin's eyes fluttered open, and he saw Will's face bent close over his. His shirt was off, and someone was wrapping a bandage around his shoulder.

"It's not a serious wound," the captain said from behind him. "Your cape must have slowed the arrow."

"Here it is," Warrenton said, producing a perfect arrow with a peacock feather. Robin sat up straighter. "Keep it as a trophy," Warrenton added. "This will teach you to lag behind us in the forest!"

Soon Robin had stood and was stretching his arms, flexing his shoulder blades, and testing the wound to see how much pain it would produce. "Come see the jousts," Warrenton suggested. "The archery contest comes later. You can decide then if you're up to it."

They walked to a set of wooden stands, decorated with red and yellow silk banners and flags, constructed in a circle around a large meadow. They slipped into a box reserved for the family of the Squire just as a blare of trumpets brought the crowd to its feet.

"The Sheriff!" a shrill-voiced woman behind them shouted. And soon the whole crowd was

chanting, "The Sheriff! The Sheriff!" as the over-weight official entered the stands.

He moved slowly, soaking up every ounce of attention. He waved and nodded with many flourishes as he moved to his box and then stood there, receiving applause for several minutes, before he finally sat with a thud.

"How the crowd adores him," Robin said to Warrenton.

"No, the crowd only cheers to keep him happy," Warrenton sneered. "He can make life miserable for the poor citizens of Nottingham," he added. "Believe me, he has done it in the past."

Beside the Sheriff sat a plain-faced young woman, her ash-white cheeks blemished with pink scars. Her hair, parted in the center and pulled behind her ears into a bun was the color of dead grass. She, too, had smiled and waved at the people, holding high her pointed nose. As she sat, she fussed with her skirt and jerked her head from right to left in a nervous twitch that reminded Robin of a chicken.

Robin asked Warrenton who she was.

"His daughter," he answered. "She fancies herself someone royal."

"A royal pain, no doubt!"

Soon the jousts began, and Robin was captivated. The knights, dressed in heavy armor, charged with all their might, thrusting their lances at each other's chests and heads. The crowd groaned as each man fell, and cheered as each new contender won his match.

After awhile Robin noticed another young woman. She was sitting, with a man who appeared to be her father, in a box below them and to their right. Her hair hung in gentle raven curls around her face and down her back. Her features were perfect, Robin thought. When she laughed, her blue eyes sparkled like the waves on a lake. She applauded with delicate hands as each new rider won his match. Her lips formed a perfect rose-colored circle when she smiled. Her dress was a deeper shade of the same rose, with a collar of pure-white lace.

Robin was torn between watching the jousts and looking at her. "Warrenton," he said, trying to sound casual. "Who is the couple who sits in that box?" He pointed to the man and the beautiful girl.

"Fitzwater," Warrenton finally remembered. "Neville Fitzwater and his daughter."

"And her name?" Robin pressed him.

"Marian, I believe," Warrenton said, keeping his eye on the jouster in the ring.

"Marian," Robin repeated. He thought it was a beautiful name.

Many knights had been disqualified when a rider dressed in red entered the circle. "Geoffrey!" Robin whispered. He controlled his horse with ease, and seemed to spur the animal to faster speeds than any other Robin had seen. His lance never wavered as he aimed it at his opponents. He won against one, then a second, and then a third challenger.

With each victory the crowd's roar grew. He felled a fourth, and finally a fifth rider, and

89

the crowd's cries and applause thundered from the stands. They stood and cheered as he rode in a circle before them. And then he stopped in front of the Sheriff's box to receive the honorary crown of victory, woven from ivy branches and decorated with daisies.

The Scarlet Knight took the wreath and galloped around the circle, displaying it on his lance held upright. And then he trotted his horse back to the box and offered the prize to the Sheriff's sharp-nosed daughter. She stood to receive it and placed it on her head, grinning at the applauding crowd.

"She tries to act surprised," Warrenton said snidely. "But this is how it always goes. The winner always gives the ivy crown to the Sheriff's daughter."

The Scarlet Knight rode to the place where Robin sat. He lifted his visor for only an instant, and smiled at Robin. "Meet me at the city gate after the tournament," he said.

"I will!" Robin answered. "You can be sure of it!"

Next came the archery contest. "Now it's your turn," Warrenton told Robin. "You will compete for the Sheriff's golden arrow. And remember, the same tradition follows this competition," Warrenton explained. "The winner gives his prize to the Sheriff's daughter."

But Robin turned toward the ring. "We'll see about that," he said as he marched onto the field.

Will followed him to the row of archers in the center of the field. The trumpeters played a fanfare. Robin and Will were examining his arrows, looking for the perfect one. "The peacock-feathered arrow!" Robin said, as he saw it among his others. "Wouldn't those outlaws like to know they helped me win the contest?" He and Will laughed.

One of the heralds stood to announce the first archer. He was a red-haired fellow with a mole on the end of his nose. His arrow missed the bull's-eye by three inches. He uttered an oath and broke an arrow over his knee as he stomped off the field.

Two more archers followed; one came close to the bull's eye, and the next missed it by only an inch. Then it was Robin's turn.

"Robin of Locksley," the herald shouted above the chatter of the crowd.

Robin looked into the stands and saw that the raven-haired Fitzwater maiden had her eyes fixed on him. His heart pounded. He glanced at Warrenton, who smiled and nodded at him, and then Robin took his stance. As he concentrated on the target, he was able to relax. He pulled his bow tight and released the arrow. It flew, straight and sure, piercing the center of the target with a thud.

"A bull's-eye!" Will said, and he jumped into the air.

"A bull's-eye!" Warrenton shouted from his seat.

"A bull's-eye!" said the Fitzwater maiden, and clapped with dainty hands.

Robin smiled and bowed as the whole crowd erupted with applause.

And then they grew silent again as the next archer took his place. "A better arrow than the last time I saw you shoot," he said to Robin, who looked up with a start.

He recognized the voice, but the face was darker, and it sported a beard.

"William of Cloudesley," the herald shouted.

Robin looked more closely. The face had been stained, probably with berry juice. And the beard wasn't real either. It looked as if he had glued horse hair onto his face!

"We'll see who wins this round," the archer said, with a cocky grin.

It was Will-o-the-Green!

Robin watched with wonder as the upstart quickly strung his bow and shot his arrow, hardly pausing to size up the target. His arrow, too, flew straight and certain to the perfect center of its mark!

The crowd came to its feet a second time, with an equally enthusiastic ovation.

The scorekeepers called it a tie, but Robin didn't care. He was thrilled with the chance to show Will-o-the-Green his newly developed skill as a bowman.

Half the competitors had been eliminated by the end of the first round. After they completed a second round, only five remained. Robin and "William of Cloudesley" were tied with the highest scores. They were the last two archers to shoot in the final round.

The day had started warm and humid, but now a cool breeze was stirring from the east. "Don't let the wind ruin your shot," Will Stutely said to Robin.

"I'm not worried," Robin answered. "Warrenton has prepared me for this."

When his turn came, Robin put Will-o-the-Green and the Fitzwater maiden out of his mind. He waited to measure the strength of the breeze. He let his arrow fly, again scoring a perfect bull's-eye.

Will-o-the-Green stepped to his place and concentrated harder than he had before. He aimed and released his shot, just as an unexpected draft gusted across the field. His shot was sure, but the wind was stronger, and Will-o-the-Green's arrow landed one-half inch from the center of the target.

"The winner is Robin of Locksley!" the herald shouted. But the crowd had already burst into a roar of applause.

Robin saw that the Fitzwater maiden was standing and cheering with the rest of them, and Warrenton had run out of the stands to congratulate him.

"You won it this time." It was Will-o-the-Green, smiling beneath his fake beard. "But not the next," he said, as he shook Robin's hand. He turned and ran off the field just as Warrenton arrived.

"Locks-ley! Locks-ley!" The crowd was chanting and clapping their hands.

Robin turned toward the Sheriff, who was standing in his box. His daughter was beside him, smiling beneath a pointed nose, clutching a blue velvet pillow with her bony hands.

Robin marched to them and bowed slightly.

The Sheriff took a deep breath, and raised his voice to address the crowd. "This Robin of Locksley has proved himself the finest archer of all who entered our magnificent competition," he shouted. "Therefore, I, the Sheriff of Nottingham, to prove my goodness to the people of this city, and to promote good sport for all, do award him a most valuable prize, the prize of the golden arrow."

The Sheriff gestured toward the velvet pillow in his daughter's outstretched hands. Nestled in the center was the prize, gleaming in the afternoon sun. The woman twitched her head and smiled at the crowd as she extended the pillow toward Robin.

He bowed and gently took the golden charm while the crowd continued to chant and clap. He clasped the treasure in his right hand and turned on his heel toward the

Fitzwater couple. In just six strides he stood before Maid Marian.

"I give my prize to you," he said to her, and he stretched his hand over the railing. She blushed as she glanced at her father, who nodded his approval, and she extended delicate fingers to receive the arrow. "Take it," Robin said, "for you have already taken my heart."

Now the crowd was on its feet again. "Bravo, Locks-ley!" they chanted.

The Sheriff stared in wide-eyed anger at the scene, while his daughter turned and stomped out of the stand.

Robin didn't notice. He could only see the maiden Marian. He could only remember the touch of her fingers brushing against his as she took the arrow.

He did not pay attention to the Sheriff.

He did not hear the crowd.

And he did not see the admiration and curiosity on the face of her father as he watched the whole scene from his seat.

CHAPTER 8

The Friends

Five riders—Robin, Geoffrey, Warrenton, Will Stutely, and Will-o-the-Green— laughed and celebrated their victories as they rode down the road out of Nottingham.

But the sting in Robin's shoulder wouldn't let him forget the problem with the outlaws in the forest. Geoffrey had almost dismissed the information Robin had given him about the two traitors out to get him. "Don't worry, Robin. I can take care of myself." Robin wasn't convinced. How did he know they wouldn't take care of him first?

Then there was the matter of Will-o-the-Green. Robin hadn't even told Warrenton the identity of their new pal, and he didn't think he should.

Yet for some reason, Robin had decided he liked the confident outlaw. He was able—that was for sure. Robin wondered if he would beat him again in another archery contest—especially without the help of an unexpected breeze.

And he was fair. A lesser man would have demanded a rematch or at least complained about how Robin won the prize.

Most of all he was likable. Will-o-the-Green told the most jokes, and the funniest, as they rode together through the woods.

Robin also tried to think of something· he could do or some words he could say to get Geoffrey and the Squire together. Robin did not care about the Squire's inheritance. But how could he tell his uncle that without making him angry—perhaps for the rest of their lives?

"I must thank you again for all you've done for me," Geoffrey said, interrupting Robin's worry.

"We will do anything—anytime," Warrenton said.

"You know you can trust us completely," Robin added. Maybe now he could convince Geoffrey to go talk with his father.

"I believe that," Geoffrey answered quickly. "That is why I want to take you into my confidence." Robin decided not to interrupt.

"I want to explain the reason for my red trappings at the joust," Geoffrey said. "You see, it was a signal. There was a contact—a spy—at the tournament."

"A spy? Who?" asked Robin.

"It doesn't matter," said Geoffrey. "The contact was watching to see what color I wore in the tournament. If I wore red, it meant that I had found a friend to work with us in Prince John's campaign against the King. If I wore black, it meant that I had failed to recruit such a friend. By now, the prince should have the word that we have enlisted an effective ally."

"Well," Robin said. "Who is he?"

As they approached a crosspath, Geoffrey reined his horse to a halt. "That friend is with us just now," he said. He nodded toward Will-o-the-Green!

"But—" Robin stammered. "How—when did you—" He turned to Warrenton, who only smiled at him. "Did you know about this?"

"Yes, Robin," he said calmly.

"And do you—do you know *who* this is?"

"Of course, Robin," the old servant chuckled. "You don't think I could be fooled by such a crude cover-up, do you?"

"But, the Squire—"

"I have not betrayed the Squire, Robin," said Warrenton. "But I cannot be disloyal to his son, my younger master, either."

"You, too, must keep my confidence, Robin." Geoffrey looked straight into Robin's face, trying to read his expression.

"You can trust me," Robin said. "But I cannot fight against my mother's brother."

"I understand that," Geoffrey answered. "It is enough for you to keep secret what you know."

Robin stared up the road toward Gamewell. "I guess it will be quite impossible for me to get you and your father together, won't it?"

"Quite," Geoffrey answered.

"Imagine … the son of the Squire plotting against the King in the company of Sherwood's bandits—and both of them helped by the Squire's own servant!"

"But, Robin," Geoffrey replied. "Lest you think you're better than me, don't forget you, too, have a friend among Sherwood's robbers."

"I never wanted to be better than you," said Robin. "I wanted only to be your friend, as well as your cousin."

Geoffrey extended his hand. "And so you are, Robin."

Robin shook his hand firmly. "And so I am." He turned to Will-o-the-Green. "And am I your friend?"

The self-confident rascal smiled brightly at Robin. "Forever!" he said. "But don't expect to beat me the next time we shoot together!"

They laughed and said farewell as Geoffrey and Will-o-the-Green turned down the cross-road and traveled away, into the woods.

Robin looked forward to the next time he would shoot with Will. But he couldn't know now that they wouldn't shoot for fun then.

CHAPTER 9

The Warning

❧━━❦━━❧

The Squire didn't smile as Robin and Warrenton and Will dismounted inside the Gamewell castle. "Robin," he said urgently. "I have bad news."

"What is it?" Robin could see tragedy in the man's eyes. "My mother? My father? It's my father, isn't it? What's wrong? Tell me what's wrong!"

"Just calm down," the Squire answered. "We received word after noon that he was gored by a stag. That's all we know. We don't know how badly he's hurt."

"Where's my mother?"

"She's already left, with six of my men, to be with your father."

"I must join her," Robin said, and turned back toward his horse.

The Squire caught his sleeve. "There's no sense in leaving now. It's almost nightfall, and the woods are full of robbers. Wait till morning. I'll send guards to go with you, too."

The roosters were crowing as Robin, the Squire, and several servants, including Warrenton, left Gamewell the next day. Montfichet had ordered six donkeys laden with any kind of gift or help that he thought his sister and her husband could need.

But by the time they got to Locksley, Robin's father needed none of it.

Eleanor Fitzooth stood in the yard to greet him. He could tell as he came close that she had been crying.

"Mother!"

"Oh, Robin," she said as she ran to his arms. "He's gone, Robin. He's gone." He held her close as she wept against his chest. Robin trembled inside when he realized there was nothing he could do.

Nothing he could do to bring his father back to life. Nothing he could do to keep his mother from crying. Nothing he could do to get rid of the heavy rock-like pain that was settling in his stomach. Nothing he could do to control his own tears that spilled out now, even though he wanted no one to see them.

After three days of non-stop activity, this morning there was nothing Robin could do. And he hated it.

But by the end of the next day, he knew what he wanted to do. The burial was over. Robin sat alone with his uncle at the same table where he had discussed the Nottingham Fair with his father.

"I want to take his place as Ranger of Locksley," he told him.

"Why, of course," the Squire answered. "I knew you would decide this."

"Uncle, will you speak for me to the King?"

"No, Robin," he answered. "That's not how it works. The Sheriff goes to the King with his recommendation for the appointment."

"The Sheriff," said Robin, remembering the fat man's outrage when Robin had given the golden arrow to Maid Marian at the fair.

"Don't worry," the Squire said. "It's only a formality. Your family has owned this property for years. Your father served half a lifetime as ranger at this post. It only makes sense that you should take his place here."

Robin hoped he was right. But he couldn't feel good about his future resting in the hands of that pompous official in Nottingham.

"I will take a letter to the Sheriff tomorrow," Montfichet offered. "I'd take up my father's duties as soon as I could, if I were you. You'll have official word soon enough."

The man left early the next morning, with all of his servants except Warrenton. "I need

him," Robin had said. "Your sister needs him." The Squire agreed quickly.

It was almost noon, almost time for lunch, when the Friar returned to check on the grieving family. Eleanor invited him to eat with them, which he did after a mild protest. After the meal, he suggested to Robin that the two of them walk together in the woods.

"The Squire is a fine man," the priest said, after they'd gone a few paces.

"Fine, indeed," Robin replied, with no emotion.

"Be sure that you do not cross him, Robin," the priest said. "Be sure that you do not push him. His mind is set, I think, about the issue of the inheritance."

"I will not take what is not mine!" Robin said, pausing after each word.

"Yes, yes, I know, I know," the priest said gently. "Just go slowly. Give the man a chance to decide for himself. I believe that he still loves his son. I believe that, down deep in his heart, where he doesn't even know it's there, the Squire wants to welcome his son back home."

"And I believe that will never happen," Robin said.

The Friar stopped walking and touched Robin's arm.

"What do you know, Robin?" He looked straight into the young man's eyes. Robin said nothing, so the priest continued. "Some say that the Scarlet Knight was really Geoffrey Montfichet." Robin didn't blink. "Some say that he's hiding in these very woods, hooked up with none other than the bandit Will-o-the-Green." Robin didn't answer. "What do you say, Robin?"

Robin turned to walk back toward the house. "I say you should give more time to your prayers and a little less to the gossip of Nottingham!" Robin answered.

"Alright. Alright!" The priest raised his voice in a way Robin had seldom heard.

"That's fine, Robin of Locksley! But let me tell you, for your own good, you'll be sorry if you make George Montfichet your enemy! And you'll be sorry if you try to deceive him!"

Robin stopped and turned back toward the priest. "Deceive him?"

The priest came close to Robin and lowered his voice. "I saw you, Robin. I saw you take Will Stutely and sneak away from the Gamewell castle in the middle of the night. I heard you talking with him and Warrenton in the courtyard after everyone else was asleep." Robin's eyes widened, and he grabbed the priest by the shoulders. "What were you doing, Robin? Where did you go?"

Robin released the priest and looked at the ground. "God help me, Father." His voice thickened and weakened. "God help me!"

The priest looked calm once again. "He will, Robin," he said. "He will. Just make sure you do everything you can to help yourself."

The Arrest

In the days that followed, Robin busied himself with the duties of the Ranger. All day, every day, in the woods and around the house, he worked as hard and as long as he could.

And in the evenings he sat and stared into the forest. Sometimes he imagined that he saw his father walking from the woods toward him. But it was only a dream. Dreams and memories occupied Robin in the nighttime. But during each day, he worked.

He was working when he heard horses in the forest, about two weeks after his father's death. "Warrenton!" he called from the roof of the house, where he was patching a leak.

"They come from the direction of Nottingham," Warrenton answered from the ground, where he was holding Robin's ladder.

Robin scrambled down the ladder, grabbed his bow and a quiver of arrows, and stood ready when ten riders came into view. At the lead was John Ford.

Robin relaxed and smiled as the forester dismounted and walked toward him. "Captain Ford! What a surprise!" Robin extended his hand, and the captain shook it without speaking. His face was serious, and his manner was all business. "Captain, what brings you here? Can we get you some refreshment?" He turned to call toward the house, but Ford interrupted.

"That won't be necessary, Fitzooth," he said, as he opened a leather pouch on his saddle. "I have with me a pronouncement from the Sheriff of Nottingham." He pulled out a scroll and uncurled it.

Warrenton stood beside Robin on the one side. Will Stutely had come to join them on the other. Robin's mother stood close to the house.

Ford's men did not dismount, but formed a semicircle behind him as he began to read. "To Robin Fitzooth of Locksley, from the King's Sheriff at Nottingham," Ford began. Robin smiled and glanced back at his mother. This was the announcement his uncle had promised! Robin hadn't expected the official word so soon!

"By this document, with all the powers invested in me by our monarch, King Henry himself, I do name the Ranger of that portion of the King's forest known as Locksley." Robin's heart began to beat faster.

"Let all men know from this day forward that John Ford of Nottingham shall serve in this important post, to protect the King's interest in the forest." Robin gasped. Ford's cheeks had slightly flushed, but he kept on reading, without looking up. "Furthermore, by my decree,

Eleanor and Robin Fitzooth, by the first day of July in the year of our Lord, one thousand, one hundred, and eighty-eight, shall vacate the premises designated as the Ranger's home so that my duly appointed Ranger may live there."

"What is the meaning of this?" Robin tore the parchment from Ford's hand. "This is ridiculous. Is this some sort of a joke?"

"I assure you that this is no joke," Ford said.

"But this is impossible," Robin shouted. "This house belongs to my father! Everyone knows that. I have been performing the Ranger's duties—I am the only one qualified to be the Ranger! I—"

"You have nothing to say about it," Ford interrupted. "This decision is the Sheriff's alone. You are to return with us today to face charges of cooperating with outlaws."

"What?"

"Don't act so surprised. You have brazenly shot peacock-feathered arrows at the Nottingham tournament. Everyone knows who

makes such arrows. Only one of Will-o-the-Green's men could own such a weapon."

"But he had only one such arrow," Warrenton interrupted. "It had been shot at Robin, by one of the outlaws in the forest!" He touched Robin's shoulder. "Robin, go get the arrow. I told you to keep it as a trophy."

"We used the arrow," Will said with a groan. "It was one of the best in Robin's quiver. We knew it would help him win!"

Warrenton glared at Stutely before turning back toward the captain. "Well, there, you see? That explains it! It was only one arrow. I can assure you you'll find no other like it here."

"Enough of this!" For the first time Ford raised his voice. "Now if you'll come with me, Fitzooth—"

"I'm going nowhere!" Robin said. But instantly Ford's men drew their swords.

"Robin," Warrenton said slowly. "Perhaps you should go." He glanced at Robin, and then at Will. "Go with them, through the forest, back to Nottingham." Robin looked confused. "You can't accomplish anything here. What good would bloodshed do? You must talk with the Sheriff, not this forester. And we'll send word to your uncle and see what say he can have in all of this."

"Yes, Robin," Will agreed. "Go with them. It's the best thing for you to do."

Robin slumped. He had been defeated. How could he fight against armed foresters and argue with his own servants too?

With hardly a word, he mounted one of the forester's horses. And in two minutes they were gone, galloping through the woods toward Nottingham.

Robin's mother was weeping by the house. "Warrenton!" she cried. "What have you done? We'll never see him again!"

"Don't worry, my lady," he said. "We will see him again before dusk!" He turned toward Stutely. "Will, prepare two horses at once! You and I must pay a visit to Will-o-the-Green!"

CHAPTER 11

The Ambush

The day was hot and still. The grass along the road was dead, and the horses' hooves raised clouds of dust.

Robin felt a trickle of sweat running along his right sideburn. But he could not reach to wipe it away, because his hands were tied to the saddle of the horse he was riding.

His shoulders ached. The leather rope rubbed a raw spot on his wrists. His seat was sore from riding for more than three hours. And it seemed that Captain Ford would not stop until they got clear to Nottingham.

"When will we rest?" Robin's voice was weak and flat.

"Sometimes we never do," the guard who rode beside him answered. He was a small man, older than Robin. His arms and legs were skinny, like young maples growing in the woods. His brown hair gave way to bushy, handle-shaped sideburns that were snowy white. They made his face seem even thinner and more wrinkled than it was.

The man had chattered on and on, almost from the moment of their fast departure from Locksley. He treated Robin more like a long-lost relative than an outlaw.

"Our captain is a hard driver," he was saying now. "Yes, indeed, I've seen him go for hours without so much as even taking a drink."

At the mention of water, Robin swallowed hard, but all he tasted was dust and his own salty sweat, dripping off his mustache.

"And what about you?" Robin said. "Aren't you ready for a drink by now?"

"Well, I suppose I am, although I hadn't—" Then he took a look at Robin and pulled both of their horses to a stop. "I say, man, you're the one who needs some water!"

He produced a bulging canvas pouch and offered it to Robin without taking a drink himself. The other riders did not stop. "We'll fall behind," Robin said between gulps.

"Aah, it doesn't matter," the small forester said. "We'll catch up soon enough." He had untied Robin's hands. "Say, there," he said when he saw how raw Robin's wrists were. "We're takin' the skin off, aren't we?" Robin didn't answer but only took another drink. The forester eyed him carefully. He looked up the road and back at Robin. "What would you say if we just left those hands untied?" he asked.

Robin raised his head, and the forester looked him straight in the eye. "I'd say that was very kind of you, sir," Robin answered.

"Alright, then," the man answered. "We can't have you bleedin' before the Sheriff of Nottingham, now, can we?"

They took off down the road again, at a slower gait than they had been trotting before. And as they rode the man kept talking.

Robin was somewhat revived by the drink, and he listened now with some interest to the man's gabbing. He learned that he was single. He had married once, but his wife had died of the plague. They had no children. After many years with many jobs, he had joined the King's foresters only last year.

"And how do you like doing the bidding of the Sheriff of Nottingham?" Robin asked.

"I love the forest," the man answered. "Even in the winter … I don't mind the cold. I love the quiet, the animals, the clean air…."

"And the Sheriff of Nottingham?" Robin asked again. "And Captain Ford?"

The man's expression darkened. "You ask an awful lot of questions for a prisoner!" he said. And for the first time, he became quiet.

They rode in silence for several minutes. And then Robin spoke again. "What's your name, sir?"

The forester brightened. "Most folks call me Midge," he said. "It's short for 'Midget,' and they say even for a midget I'd be short!" Then he laughed at the silly play on words, and Robin chuckled too.

"I know what you mean about the forest, Midge," Robin continued. "I've been in the city, but I like the forest better. You can be yourself in the forest. In the city someone's always trying to bend you into what they want, you know what I mean?"

Midge smiled again. "I know what you mean!"

Just then they heard a shrill bugle in the woods ahead of them. "What's that?" Midge asked.

"I think I know!" Robin said. "Let's go!"

They galloped hard for only three minutes till they came around a bend to see Ford's riders scattered ahead of them.

"Outlaws!" Midge shouted.

"Friends!" Robin replied. A swarm of Will-o-the-Green's men had descended on John Ford and his group. The outlaws were swinging from the trees and knocking the foresters off their horses. Some hid in the woods and rained arrows toward several of the foresters crouching behind a log. Two were wrestling in the dirt with two of the foresters.

Ford had drawn his sword and was sparring with Will-o-the-Green himself! Will was smiling like always, but Ford gasped and heaved with each jab.

"So I see the new Ranger has met his match!" Robin called from his horse.

The shout distracted Ford for just an instant, long enough for Will to knock the weapon from the captain's hand. Just as quickly Will kicked the man in the shoulder. He fell backwards to the ground, and Will thrust his sword toward his neck.

"No, Will!" Robin screamed, and rode quickly to him.

"Aah, it was just a tweak!" Will said with a self-satisfied toss of his head. "I only meant to scare him." But still he didn't move. The captain was white-faced and panting on the ground, unable to speak because the point of the sword pressed against his Adam's apple.

By now the rest of the men were equally disabled. Some had been bound. Two were brought at knife-point toward their squirming captain. Three lay helpless on the ground,

held there by triumphant outlaws. None had been killed, but one had been wounded, and three of the outlaws were bent over him now, removing the arrow from his shoulder.

It had all happened so quickly that poor Midge hadn't had time to react. And now with every one of his friends disarmed, Midge sat on his horse stunned and sputtering.

"Just relax, Midge," Robin said with a laugh. "No one will hurt you." Two of Will's men came up behind him and pulled him off his horse.

"Speak for yourself, Robin!" Will said as he moved the tip of his sword from Ford's throat to his chest and stabbed lightly at his shirt.

"Let … me … go!" Ford gasped, and Will-o-the-Green laughed at him.

"Where shall we let him go, Robin?" Will-o-the-Green said. "Back to Locksley, so he can take your job and steal your home?"

"How did you know about that?" Robin asked. But before Will could answer, Warrenton and Will Stutely bounded out of the forest,

135

beaming from ear to ear. Robin cheered and ran toward them. They had taken a shortcut and raced to Will-o-the-Green's hideout. Warrenton knew the place, because he had met Geoffrey there, the night before the jousts.

The outlaws were emptying the forester's pouches and taking their weapons. Ford was stumbling toward his horse with the point of Will-o-the-Green's sword at his back. "You will pay for this!" Ford said, his voice shaking.

"Ah, sure," Will-o-the-Green answered with a sneer. "And if we do, now we'll have something to pay with!" He held up the captain's pouch, and poured a pile of shiny coins onto the ground. The captain mounted his horse, sputtering and swearing under his breath, and Will-o-the-Green scooped up the money.

Poor Midge was trembling between two of the outlaws. His face was as white as his sideburns. And his knobby knees almost bounced against each other. Robin looked across the clearing at him and had an idea.

"This one will be my prisoner!" he said.

"What will we do with a prisoner?" Will-o-the-Green said.

"Robin, we have business to attend to!" Warrenton said.

"What business?" Robin replied. "My business has been taken away from me! Our business is right here, in the forest, with Will-o-the-Green!"

"We must talk with the Squire," Warrenton insisted. "He can help you get to the bottom of this. There must be some mistake. He can handle that dolt of a Sheriff. We must go today!"

"Maybe," Robin said thoughtfully. He looked again at Midge. "Nevertheless, let's keep a hostage to show the Sheriff that he cannot have his way with us." He glanced at Will-o-the-Green.

"I don't like it," Will-o-the-Green said, "but I'll trust you on this." He nodded to the two guarding Midge. They pulled him across the road and pushed him toward Robin.

With loud laughter and catcalls, the outlaws tied the other foresters to their horses and sent them galloping to Nottingham.

Midge had more color in his face now, and Robin walked with him toward their horses. He had his arm on Midge's shoulder, like a friend.

"It will be alright, Midge," Robin whispered.

"I believe you, Robin," Midge said softly. "I believe you."

CHAPTER 12

The Rejection

The quartet of riders sped through the woods toward the outlaw hideout. From there they would use the secret passageway that led to the hut inside the Gamewell grounds.

Robin was exuberant. It felt good to be free again. It felt good to be in control. It felt very good to have seen the rascal John Ford humiliated. It felt good to have Midge as his new chum.

And that was how Robin viewed him. He would give Midge the choice, of course, but Robin felt sure that Midge would stay in the woods with him from this day forward.

It was almost dark, and they were close to the cave entrance to the secret path. A sudden rustling of tree branches high above them was followed by a burst of cool air. Then they heard thunder in the distance. They ignored it and kept riding, but soon the rain began, first as giant drops splashing here and there, and then as a roaring downpour.

It was a cool, refreshing relief—at first. But after ten minutes, all four of them were drenched and shivering.

Warrenton spied a huge fallen tree with a rotted-out trunk almost four feet around. "Take the hostage, and hide there," he shouted at Stutely through the noise of the storm. "Robin and I will go to Gamewell and meet you back here in the morning."

"But why can't we go on to the outlaws' hideout?" Will protested.

"And show this forester how to get there?" Warrenton shouted. "What if he escapes? He'd bring John Ford and the Sheriff of Nottingham too, and then where would our friends be?"

It was too late, and Robin was too tired to argue. He told Will to do what Warrenton said, and he and Warrenton headed deeper into the forest.

Soon the two had found the entrance to the secret passage. They cleared away the brush hiding a two-foot-wide hole and crawled inside. After wriggling through a narrow, black shaft, they came to a rock-walled room that was seven feet high. Warrenton fumbled until he found a lantern hidden there by the outlaws, and soon they were making their way through the glistening caverns by its flickering light.

Warrenton used this chance, away from Midge, to express himself to Robin. "Ford will chase you till he gets his revenge," he said. "The Sheriff already hates you for snubbing his daughter at the tournament. Now you've disgraced his captain and captured one of his foresters.

"Ford will have no choice but to chase you with a vengeance. The rest of his men will desert him if he doesn't rescue this Midge. And the Sheriff will dismiss him if he doesn't restore his honor. You've made a fool of both Ford and the Sheriff, Robin. Everyone in Nottingham will know about it. This is too big for them to ignore or forget."

"But you've forgotten my uncle," Robin finally said. "You said yourself that he would handle the Sheriff."

"That was when I was trying to talk you out of taking a prisoner. Now, I don't know what will happen."

They had reached the end of the passage. Above them were three slats covering the entrance to the hut on Gamewell grounds. The passage angled upwards, toward the slats, and Warrenton easily pushed them up into the hut. He and Robin crawled inside, and Warrenton creaked the hut's door open to look across the lawn toward the castle. It was not raining now, but the sky was cloudy and dark, and the breeze blew even cooler. The two men shivered again as they ran through the shadows, through the garden, and to the servants' door that Warrenton had used so many times before.

"Who's there?" said one of the maids as Warrenton and Robin stepped inside. She rec-

ognized them, and her eyes opened wide. "As God is my witness, look what the rain blew in! It's our master's outlaw nephew and his runaway servant!"

"Hush, woman!" Warrenton whispered. "We are neither outlaw nor runaway. Now quit your babbling and tell us where the Squire is!"

The woman looked afraid. "The last I saw 'im, 'e was in the study," she said. "But if you think I'm going to take you to see 'im, you're crazy!" She scooted down the hall away from them as Robin and Warrenton hurried toward the study.

The Squire stood with his back to the doorway at a massive, carved oak table. He was bent over a scroll spread out across the center of the table.

"Uncle?" Robin said softly.

The man stiffened and turned to scowl at them.

"How did you get here?" he said with a glare. "Where have you been? You're soaking wet and filthy dirty!" He took two steps toward Robin. "I offered you the finest clothes, the best lodging in the land, but look at you now. Is this what you want, Robin of Locksley? To wallow in the mud with the outlaws of the forest?"

"No— I— We've come to get your help. We need you to talk with the Sheriff about—"

"I've already talked with the Sheriff!" Montfichet roared. "I've talked more with the Sheriff than I ever want to talk with him again!" The Squire turned away from the two, toward an open window ahead of them. "He told me about you, Robin. He told me about the peacock-feathered arrow you shot at the tournament."

"It was only one arrow, sir, and I can explain—"

"He told me about Geoffrey." He turned back toward Robin, his eyes narrow, his cheeks turning red, his white lips trembling. "I *know* about you and Geoffrey! The Scarlet

147

Knight, indeed!" He pointed one finger at Robin. "And while I was giving you the very best that I had and promising you far more to come!"

"Sir, please calm down. I can explain everything." Robin moved toward him, but the man turned away.

"Talk's cheap, Robin," he said, and then he spun around to face him again. "I know what you *did!* Plotting against me in my own house! I won't have it, Robin. I won't have *you!*" He marched past him, toward the door to the room. "Get out! You are no son of mine! You are no *relative* of mine!" He pushed the door open, and stood in the hall to hold it. "And take this man with you," he said of Warrenton. He had not looked at him once since the two entered the room. "He reminds me of someone I once knew, but I think that man is now dead. Now get out. Get *out!*"

CHAPTER 13

The Victory

Robin and Warrenton slept in the forest, with Stutely and Midge. Will-o-the-Green's men had discovered the two hiding in the tree trunk and had brought them bread, some berries, and a flask of wine. Robin and Warrenton ate a little of it when they arrived, long after dark.

They arose early the next morning. With aching backs and broken spirits, they rode slowly to Locksley.

"What am I to do?" Robin asked Warrenton as their horses trotted along the trail.

"You cannot stay at Locksley," Warrenton told him.

"But my mother—"

"I believe your mother will be safe there," Warrenton said. "It's you the Sheriff will be chasing. And Ford will not be so bold as to oust a widow from her home."

They arrived late in the morning, in time for Robin's mother to prepare them a hearty lunch. She was disturbed and disappointed with their news from Gamewell. But she was thrilled to see Robin and know he was safe.

Their exhaustion overtook them after their stomachs were full, and they spent most of the afternoon in a deep sleep.

That evening, the four men sat and discussed their options.

"Maybe Geoffrey could help us," Robin said.

"Geoffrey has gone to France," Warrenton answered, in a flat tone.

"France?"

"Will-o-the-Green's man brought us the news when he gave us the food," Warrenton said. "But what could he do for you, anyway, Robin? "He is no better than us—a criminal and an outcast." Warrenton's voice trailed off to almost a whisper, as he lowered his head and slumped his shoulders.

Their conversation melted into a sad silence. Soon each of them stood from the table and wandered to a different corner of the Ranger's property. Midge found a puppy to play with. Will Stutely practiced tumbles and cartwheels in the yard. Robin took a knife and whittled a stick. And Warrenton sat, just sat and stared into the woods as the green grew gray with the dusk.

They were awakened the next morning by horse's hooves outside the house.

"Robin! Are you here?"

Robin hurried to the doorway to find John Berry, one of his loyal Locksley foresters, out of breath as he dismounted from his horse.

"Robin, you must leave! They're after you."

"How many?"

"Dozens of them, Robin. They're scattered all over the forest—scouting parties everywhere. And behind them whole companies of Ford's men, armed with pikes and staves as well as their bows and arrows."

By now Warrenton and Will and Midge had gathered around the forester.

"Let's go!" said Will.

"I'm with you," said Warrenton.

All of them looked at Midge at the same time. "Midge, I know you can be a big help to me," Robin said. "I know you love these woods, and I feel you're ready to be free of the likes of John Ford and the miserable Sheriff. But our lives are on the line here. I can't make you stay."

"I don't want to go back," Midge said, his expression serious. "But, Robin, I can't fight Ford's men. They're my friends—I lived with them for a year." His eyes darted between the men, and then his expression brightened. "Let me stay here. I'll guard your mother."

"It's a good plan," Robin said immediately. "I know I can trust you."

"I will protect her with my life," Midge vowed.

"Robin, we must go," Berry said urgently.

In a flash, Robin had gathered his bow and a quiver full of arrows, while Warrenton and Will Stutely did the same. Robin embraced his mother. "Don't worry," he said as he looked into her troubled eyes. "I'll be back." With tears streaming down her face, she watched them gallop into the forest.

They decided to head for Will-o-the-Green's hideout. Where else could they go to be safe? They met three other foresters in a clearing not far from Locksley, and the seven headed through the woods to find Will-o-the-Green.

All four of the foresters had vowed never to work for John Ford. They had loved and respected Hugh Fitzooth, and they were loyal to his son Robin. They would not see him put in stocks while they enjoyed their freedom with the man who imprisoned him.

They were riding on a narrow path along a ridge above a deep valley. A rock wall rose to their right, and a steep drop-off fell to their left. At the bottom of the valley a winding stream gurgled and splashed, still flooded by the rains of two days before. It would have been a peaceful place if it weren't for the fear that pounded inside Robin's head.

Their horses found their way slowly along the trail.

"How much longer to the outlaws' hiding place?" John Berry asked.

"We're not close yet," said Robin. But just then they heard noise ahead of them. Men shouted in the distance. And the clanging of metal against metal echoed through the valley.

"Off your horses!" Robin ordered. They tied the animals to saplings, and crept toward a bend in the trail.

Robin gasped as they turned the bend and saw the source of the noise below them. John

Ford and at least fifty foresters were fighting Will-o-the-Green's men in a desperate battle.

"Stay low," Robin hissed. None of the men below them saw Robin and his friends. Will's men were outnumbered, but their skill as archers kept most of Ford's men pinned behind whatever tree or rock they could find for cover.

"This way," Robin ordered, and his band crawled into the valley, above and behind Ford's men. "Now!" Robin said again, and the seven of them released a shower of arrows at the Sherwood foresters' backs.

Ford's men groaned as arrows found their mark. "Attack!" Robin shouted, and all seven stood and roared at the confused Sherwood foresters. With opponents on two sides, Ford's men began to run away from them, up the opposite side of the valley. Will-o-the-Green's men seized their advantage, and rushed from their hiding places as well, swinging hatchets, aiming arrows, and raising their voices in a frightening war cry.

"Aha!" Robin shouted as Ford's men retreated. Then his eyes fell on two among Ford's group who seemed not to belong with him. They were dressed in tattered muslin shirts. One was short, but the other was tall and thin, with a dirty gray beard. They were the traitors who had attacked Robin the day of the jousts!

"After those two!" Robin hollered to John Berry. The outlaws were desperately struggling to get up a hillside, slipping on fallen leaves, trying to pull themselves up by their hands.

Berry and two other foresters ran after them. "Halt!" Berry shouted as his foresters released a hail of arrows that thudded into the ground around the traitors.

They turned and fell down the hill, landing on their backs at John Berry's feet. He bound their hands and brought them to Robin.

"So, who do we have here?" Robin sneered. "Are these woodsmen ... or *skunks?*"

Ford's men had been completely run off. Will-o-the-Green's men chased them through the forest, keeping them running in front of a steady barrage of arrows.

Soon Will-o-the-Green met up with Robin. "Great timing," he said, flashing his smile. "I think we're done with them for awhile."

"They'll be back," Robin said grimly. "They won't give up."

Will-o-the-Green ignored the remark when he saw Robin's prisoners tied to a tree stump and guarded by John Berry. "Tom!" he shouted in surprise. "Andrew!"

"These are the two who shot at me outside Nottingham," Robin said. "I heard them plotting against Geoffrey—and against you."

Will-o-the-Green's mouth turned downward and his eyes flashed with anger. "So you think you can live with me and plot with the Sheriff too, do you?" He turned to one of his men. "Bring them here!" he ordered.

"Strip off their shirts," he told his man. "Take their hats, and their shoes, too." The man obeyed him, treating the two traitors roughly as he undressed them. "Now, tie them to two horses," Will continued, "the two worst horses you can find."

Soon the man had found two bow-backed nags and mounted each of the traitors—backwards—on one of them. "Tie their feet underneath," Will-o-the-Green said. "And then tie their backs to the horses' backs, with their faces in the animals' tails."

Andrew and Tom whimpered as rough ropes bound their bare shoulders to the horses' hind ends. They were still protesting as Will-o-the-Green's men led the horses to the stream and sent them wandering, each in a different direction, into the woods.

"Now, come with me, Robin," Will-o-the-Green said. "We've won a victory. We need to celebrate!"

CHAPTER 14

The Decision

Will-o-the-Green's men welcomed Robin and his friends with cheers and shouts. The outlaws crowded around them, slapping them on the back and shaking their hands. A fire hissed and popped in an open pit, and a giant, skinned deer was roasting over the flame.

"Come!" Will-o-the-Green gestured to Robin and the others. "Sit! We have beaten the Sheriff's scoundrel forester. Now we should eat!"

For the first time in two days, Robin smiled. He joined Will-o-the-Green and a circle of outlaws congratulating themselves for what they'd done.

John Berry and the Locksley foresters were treated like old friends. Soon each of them was laughing and talking with a different bunch of Will-o-the-Green's men.

Someone started playing a lively jig on a wooden flute, and some of the men clapped in time with the tune. A few jumped up and danced in a circle while the rest cheered and laughed. Now Will Stutely was in the center of the crowd, entertaining everyone with back flips, handstands, and cartwheels.

Even Warrenton seemed to be happy as he sat and smiled at all the activity from the shade of a giant elm. Robin spied him and came to sit beside him.

They watched together in silence for a moment before Robin spoke. "I feel like I belong here," he said to the old man. "I want to stay here."

"It's a good decision," Warrenton replied. "I will stay here with you, Robin. I, too, have nowhere else to go."

Robin looked across the clearing at John Berry and the other foresters, laughing and eating with Will-o-the-Green's men. "I believe they will want to be with us," Robin said. "We will have our freedom here. We will fight the Sheriff together, if necessary—"

"It will be necessary," Warrenton interrupted.

"We will have each other," Robin continued. "And we will be happy." He poked at the dirt with a stick.

"But I must go tell my mother what I'm doing," Robin said. "And I must give Midge the chance to join us if he wants."

Warrenton sighed. "She will probably be safer without him there," he said. He looked at Robin again. "When will you go to Locksley?"

"At first light," he answered.

"Then I shall go with you," Warrenton said.

The party continued into the night, but Robin slipped away early and fell into a deep sleep. The woods were gray and still the next morning, as he and Warrenton left the camp.

They arrived at Locksley to find Midge standing guard outside Robin's house, like a toy knight at attention by the door. Midge and Warrenton stayed in the yard while Robin went inside to talk with his mother.

"You cannot stay here," she said after he told her his plan. "I understand that. I have many friends. If John Ford—" Her voice broke and she looked down at her hands. "If John Ford seizes this house," she continued, "there are many places I could go."

"You are very brave, Mother," he said, taking both of her hands in his.

"Your father taught me to be brave," she said with a small smile, "just as he taught you."

"I will come back," he told her. "When you least expect it, I will sneak to Locksley to see you." They hugged in a tight embrace. And this time when he left, she did not cry.

CHAPTER 15

The Deserter

News of Robin's exploits with Will-o-the-Green spread throughout the Locksley forest. One after another, Hugh Fitzooth's foresters found Robin and asked to join him in hiding. If John Ford was to be Ranger of Locksley, he would need to recruit a whole new regiment of foresters!

Some of the men Robin knew well. They had served with his father since Robin was a boy. John Berry was one of these. So was Much the Miller. No one knew if Much had ever actually worked as a miller or not. His father had, but Much had patrolled the forest with Robin's father since he could remember.

"I've always known one day I would ride with you," he told Robin. "I'll not serve some Sheriff's hireling who's trying to steal your place!"

Middle the Tinker was younger, and newer to Locksley. He had a one-room house and workshop in the village not far from Robin's home. Middle could mend a harness, repair a saddle, fashion a chain, or make a rope. But more than all his odd jobs, he enjoyed riding through the woods with Fitzooth and his men.

The same story was repeated over and over. In the first two weeks after Robin told his mother good-bye, more than twenty foresters joined him in hiding.

Even Friar Tuck came to Robin's side. "God will not bless a man who's acting like this Sheriff," he told Robin glumly. He did not move from his simple home at Copmanhurst, but his eyes and ears took in any shred of news that could help Robin stay alive in the forest.

Robin's group was so large that Will-o-the-Green's camp couldn't hold them. So Will's men helped Robin's men build a new hideout. Within a month Robin was leader of a band of men as able and crafty as Will-o-the-Green's had ever been.

But there was no conflict or competition between the two camps, mainly because Will-o-the-Green and Robin trusted each other so completely. Each of them had saved the other's life, and they were equal marksmen. They decided together about who would work where, and when. And Will was glad for Robin to take a portion of their loot to help the poor villagers of Locksley who couldn't afford the heavy taxes laid on them by the Sheriff of Nottingham.

Robin could only wish that the men in his camp always got along together so well. Taking charge of so many, day in and day out, was something new to Robin. Will-o-the-Green kept telling him that arguing and jealousy among the men was normal. "They like to shoot. They like to brag. They like to fight," he said to Robin. "If they were a bunch of mild-mannered pansies who always did what everybody told 'em, they'd be no good to you here!"

Robin was learning. He was learning to hear both sides of an argument before he decided who was right. He was learning to let the men solve their own disagreements whenever possible.

But one of his band continued to trouble him.

His name was John Little Nailor. Everyone called him Little John, precisely because he was so big! He was a lumbering hulk of a man, almost seven feet tall, who weighed close to three hundred pounds.

His hair was dark and curly. And his eyebrows made a thick, black hedge across his wide forehead. Each of his hands was as thick as a loaf of bread and as strong as a knight's shield. His arms were round as a tree and firm as a horse, and he could get his way with almost anyone, just by bullying them.

Usually he chose to be gentle, but when he was angry, he pushed, he punched, he shouted, or he threatened. He was at the center of more trouble than everyone else in the camp combined, and Robin didn't know what to do.

It's true that Robin was the one man Little John never challenged. Robin and his father had rescued him once, years ago. It was springtime, and Little John fell into a flooded stream. Sputtering and splashing in the rushing water, he couldn't get out, even though it wasn't over his head. The two Fitzooths tossed him a rope and threw him a staff so he could pull himself to the muddy shore.

"You saved my life. You saved my life!" the giant had bellowed as he engulfed Robin and his father in soggy bear hugs. "Ask me anything. Tell me anything. I owe you my life. I owe you my life!" From that day till now, Little John had been convinced that Robin and his father were his salvation. Robin tried to use that to his advantage now.

The giant stood before Robin, looking at his hat in his hands and swaying slightly from left to right. "Little John, there has been another complaint," Robin began softly. "Will Stutely says you pushed him into a campfire while he was practicing his headstand. Is that true?"

The man's head raised on his thick neck. Robin could see the hurt in Little John's eyes. "He called me a name!" he answered.

"If Will Stutely called you a name, that was wrong," Robin said calmly. "But, John, you can't tromp through this camp trying to solve your problems by pushing people around. John, did you push Will Stutely into the fire?"

His face was defiant now. He was breathing deeply, and his cheeks were red. "Yes."

Robin sighed. "Then you shall not ride with the men on the patrols for the next week. While you're sitting here in the camp, I want you to think about how you can control yourself better with the other men. Do you understand?"

"I understand all right!" he said, and he kicked the dirt with his massive left foot. "I understand how it is in this lousy camp!" He turned and stomped away from Robin, muttering with each step. He picked up a basketful of fruit and smashed it on the ground as he passed one man's tent. And he kicked dirt into a small fire burning in front of another.

Robin called after him. But the man didn't stop, he didn't turn, and he didn't answer.

At roll call the next morning, no one answered when Robin called, "John Little Nailor."

"Warrenton, Little John is gone!"

The old man's eyes crinkled. "Is that bad— or good?" he asked, and the men burst into laughter.

Robin turned away and admitted to himself that he didn't really know how to answer Warrenton's question.

CHAPTER 16

The Search

R obin was sure Little John would be back. And so was everyone else in the camp.

"Where would he go?" Warrenton asked.

"Who else would have him?" Will Stutely pointed out.

"We're the only family he knows," John Berry told Robin.

This kind of talk satisfied Robin for one week, and then a second. But by the middle of the third week with no sign of John Little Nailor, Robin began to wonder if he'd ever see him again. After four weeks, Robin was worried that something awful had happened to the oversized man.

He had sent several search parties into the woods to see if Little John was hiding—or hurt—in the forest. They had found nothing. Two of Robin's men had slipped into Locksley to see if Little John had shown up there. But he hadn't. And Friar Tuck could tell them nothing.

"Maybe he's in Nottingham," Robin said to Will-o-the-Green one morning.

Will-o-the-Green pursed his lips and raised his eyebrows. "It's the only place you haven't looked," he agreed.

"We should search for him there," Robin decided. But then his shoulders sank. "But where would we begin? And who can we trust?"

Will-o-the-Green tapped two fingers on the table where they sat. Robin sensed that he knew something he wasn't telling him. "Will?" He kept tapping. "Will! Tell me!"

Will-o-the-Green sat up and looked Robin straight in the eye. "Robin, we have a contact in Nottingham…. A friend…. A spy."

Robin didn't know there were any secrets between them. "Really," he said slowly.

"Actually, I haven't thought about the man much lately. We haven't talked with him in months."

"Who is this spy?"

"His name is Fitzwater. Neville Fitzwater. He is a warden in Nottingham."

Robin's mind was racing. "Fitzwater! He has a daughter!"

"A beautiful daughter, in fact!"

"Yes! Of course, I've seen him. I've met her. Well, not really met her." Robin had stood, and he was pacing in front of Will-o-the-Green. "She was at the tournament. Fitzwater's daughter is the one I gave the golden arrow to!"

"Instead of the Sheriff's beak-nosed old maid!"

Robin seemed seized with a new idea. "You say this Fitzwater is a spy?"

"He has given us information, yes. And he has taken information for us to Prince John."

"*He* is the one Geoffrey mentioned that day we rode home from the jousts!"

"Yes."

"You know you can trust him?" Robin asked.

"With my life."

"Then he can tell us if Little John is in Nottingham!"

"It's a brilliant idea, Robin." Will stood up. "I'll send a man to Nottingham tonight. We can have an answer back by tomorrow."

Robin stopped pacing. "I want to go," he said.

"You?"

"I want to talk to Fitzwater myself. I want to find Little John on my own."

"And you want to see Fitzwater's daughter again, don't you?" Will-o-the-Green was smiling. "Let's see now, what was her name?"

"Marian," Robin answered quickly. "Her name is Marian."

"Alright," Will-o-the-Green answered. "You shall go. Tonight. But you must be very careful, Robin."

It was dusk when Robin walked into the city dressed as a beggar. The hood on his tunic was over his head, covering his face. Will-o-the-Green had told him how to find Fitzwater's house by snaking through back streets and alleys.

Soon he was at Fitzwater's back door. He recognized it by a special carved leaf design. Will-o-the-Green had showed him what to look for. He glanced to his left and then to his right, to make sure no one was watching. Then he knocked, three times in a row, followed by a pause and a single knock, then another pause followed by three more knocks. Will-o-the-Green had taught him the signal.

Nothing happened. Robin's heart was pounding. His head was sweating under the hood. He tried the secret knock again. This time, the door creaked open. Robin saw a pair of eyes on the other side.

He raised the two outside fingers of his left hand—another secret signal. "I've been sent from the forest," he said, repeating the password Will had taught him.

"And do the deer run wild in the forest?" the voice asked him.

"Only as long as the King allows," Robin answered, completing the signal.

The door opened wide enough for Robin to slip inside. He stood before a pinch-faced woman with short wisps of gray and brown hair.

"I have come to see Master Fitzwater," he said, once she closed the door behind him.

"Of course," she answered, and she led him through the kitchen where they were standing in a hallway toward the front of the house. "Wait here."

"And, so, I am blessed with a visitor from the greenwood," said Fitzwater soon, walking quickly down a large stairway that dominated the hall. Robin glanced up to see a trim, handsome gentleman. His hair was the blue-gray of a knight's armor, except for the white at his temples. His jacket was of green velvet, and he wore a wide gold band on the middle finger of his right hand. He casually raised the two outside fingers of his left hand as he came to the bottom of the stairs. Robin repeated the gesture without comment.

"I am Robin Fitzooth," he said. Fitzwater shook his hand firmly.

"I recognize you even under that hood," Fitzwater replied. "I believe I cheered for you at the tournament not long ago."

"Thank you, sir," Robin said.

"Come in." They were standing alone now. The servant had quietly disappeared. "Sit down," Fitzwater said, motioning to two oak chairs in a small room off the hallway. "You have news?"

"No, sir," Robin began. "We were hoping to get some news from you."

Fitzwater folded his hands and looked relaxed as Robin told him about his missing man.

"I know of no outlaw who has taken up residence in Nottingham," Fitzwater answered. "What does this man look like?"

"He's big. He's a giant. His name is John Little Nailor, and everyone calls him Little John!"

"Does he have black, curly hair and bushy eyebrows?"

"Yes! That's him! Have you seen him?"

Fitzwater frowned. "He works as a kitchen helper for the Sheriff of Nottingham!"

"For the Sheriff! What can this mean?" Robin was agitated.

"I don't know," Fitzwater said with a serious expression. "Don't be too concerned, Robin. Maybe it doesn't mean anything."

"I knew he was upset," said Robin. "But I never imagined he would betray me."

"You don't know that he has," said Fitzwater. "Let me investigate. I can find out why the Sheriff hired him and what he knows about him."

"No. I want to see him for myself." Robin's fear had turned to anger.

"Robin, that's very dangerous."

"I can't go back to the forest without knowing what I'm facing." Robin stood up and began pacing the floor.

"You can stay here as long as—"

"And I will not rot inside this house while someone else does my work for me!"

"Father?" It was a soft female voice. Robin looked up to see Fitzwater's daughter standing in the doorway. Her hands were folded, and her head was cocked. To Robin she looked like a fragile flower.

"Marian!" Fitzwater stood and reached his hand out to her. He smiled at her.

"Father, I heard voices, and I—"

"Marian, we have a guest," he said, standing by her side with his arm around her shoulders. "Perhaps you remember Master Robin Fitzooth?"

She looked surprised. "Yes," she said. "Oh, yes." And her right hand went to her neck where a gleaming golden arrow hung from a delicate chain.

"Master Robin will be joining us for dinner," Fitzwater said. Robin hardly heard him. He stood speechless at the sight of Maid Marian. She was more beautiful than he remembered.

191

Her blue eyes flashed, and she blushed slightly to see Robin staring at her. "I'll make sure we've set an extra place for him," she said, and she slipped out of the room.

"Come," said Fitzwater, and now he moved to put an arm across Robin's shoulders. "Our problem won't seem so big after we've eaten a hearty meal."

Their dinner was simple but very good. A mutton soup, thick with vegetables, was accompanied with chewy brown bread, a round of cream-colored cheese, and sweet French wine. Fitzwater spoke freely in front of his daughter about the politics of the kingdom and the secrets of Sherwood forest.

Soon he had a plan for uncovering the mystery of the Sheriff's new worker. "We'll dress you as a butcher," he told Robin. "They sell their meat every day in the market square. I have a friend who can lend you his cart, if you like. Perhaps you'll hear some news there. Meanwhile, I'll ask questions of some people I can trust. Don't worry, Robin. We'll get to the bottom of this!"

They ate sweet, juicy apples for dessert, and soon Fitzwater retired to his chamber.

"You are wearing the golden arrow," Robin said to Marian. They sat on the same side of the table, where they had eaten their meal.

"I have worn it every day since you gave it to me," she said.

"You're— you're very beautiful," Robin said. "I have … never known a lady as … as lovely as you," he said between deep breaths.

"You're trying to flatter me," she said, and she stood from the table and moved toward the wall to straighten a tipped candle dripping wax from the sconce onto the floor.

"No!" Robin stood too. "I mean it. I have thought of you often. I wanted to see you again. I had no idea it would be so easy! I never dreamed your father was a—"

"It's all right," she said, with a defiant air. "You can say the word. He is a spy."

"He is a man who lives by the courage of his convictions," Robin said.

"That's what I admire most about him," she replied. She looked straight into Robin's face.

"I think that you, too, Robin Fitzooth, are a man who does what he thinks is right, regardless of the consequences."

"My father taught me that's the only honorable way to live," he said, and he looked deep into her eyes.

She did not move. He raised his hand to touch her cheek. She closed her eyes and moved closer to him. And then they kissed. Once, and then again they kissed.

Robin tasted the kiss later as he drifted to the bedroom Fitzwater's servant had prepared for him. He thought of the kiss as he lay sleepless in his bed till well after midnight. His mind spun with the news of the night and that kiss in the night. What did it all mean? What should he do next? Where would this all lead?

Robin didn't know, but he could not sleep for considering the possibilities.

CHAPTER 17

The Spy

"P erfect!" Fitzwater surveyed the butcher he and his servants had created.

It was Robin, of course, dressed in leggings and a blood-stained apron. Fitzwater's maid had coated Robin's hair and mustache with coal dust and grease. And Robin had tried Will-o-the-Green's old trick of darkening his skin with berry juice. He wore the same hooded tunic he had used the night before. He slipped the hood over his head to complete his disguise.

Marian giggled as she watched from the doorway of the kitchen where they worked. "The hood is the finishing touch!" she said. "I believe you should wear one all the time!"

"If you say so, then so shall it be!" Robin answered.

"Let's make it part of your name," she continued. "Robin of the Hood... Robin-o'-the-Hood... Robin Hood!"

"And why not?" Robin answered. "I am not Robin of Locksley now, for Locksley is not my home. Robin Hood—I like the sound of it!"

Fitzwater led him to the alley where a butcher's cart waited, loaded down with fresh cuts of mutton and beef. He gave Robin directions to the market square, and then shook his hand firmly. "Do not return here before dark," he said. "We will be chained in the Sheriff's prison if he finds out we're helping you."

Robin found the place where the butchers did their business and set up shop. To make sure no one recognized him, he acted like a simpleton. He talked nonsense, made up silly rhymes, and sang tunes with no melody or meaning.

No one had told him how much his meat cost, so he made up the prices as he went.

Those dressed poorly paid only a few pennies, while Robin charged the wealthy several gold pieces for the same amount.

This peculiar pricing, combined with Robin's silly chatter and loud singing, made him the center of attention in the market-place. Robin had sold all of his meat before any of the others. He learned nothing about Little John and the Sheriff, but he did discover that the Sheriff was throwing a party—that very night!—for the merchants.

He decided to try a conversation with the butcher beside him.

"I guess you can come, too, dullard," the butcher sneered at him, "although I don't know why you should be invited after only one day at the market!"

When the time came, Robin shuffled along with the others to the courtyard inside the Sheriff's castle. Robin kept his hood up and his eyes down, so that he wouldn't be recognized by any of the Sheriff's servants.

The butchers sat on benches at long tables. Servants moved among them, bringing bread and filling tankards with ale. Robin had just started eating when he saw the figure of Little John towering over a table on the other side of the courtyard.

Before long, Little John came to Robin's table, carrying two large pitchers. Robin's eyes had not been off him. When he came close, Robin raised his mug. "More. More!" he demanded in a loud, low voice. He raised his eyes to look straight at Little John who gasped when he saw him. He recognized Robin in spite of the disguise.

"I could have you put in prison!" Little John whispered in Robin's ear as he poured the ale.

"And I could do the same to you!" said Robin.

Little John moved on to the next empty mug, and by the time he got back to Robin, Robin pretended to be overcome by the strong brew. He slumped over as though he were asleep. His face rested on the table. His hood

lapped over the edge of his plate, and his loud "snoring" echoed through the courtyard.

Everyone around him was laughing. They had been making fun of him all day, and now here was something new to ridicule. "Aah, the ill-mannered buffoon," Little John muttered. "I'll clear away this piece of trash along with the rest of the dirty dishes!"

He grabbed Robin under the arms and dragged him out of the courtyard, through the kitchen, and into a walk-in pantry. "Lie there, you nasty pig!" he shouted, loud enough for the servants bustling in and out of the kitchen to hear him. "Lie there in a clean sty for once. But be quiet about it, or you'll be sleeping in the alley!" Little John pushed the door shut, leaving Robin on the floor beneath the shelves of food.

As soon as the door was latched, Robin knelt and watched from the keyhole as other servants bustled in and out of the kitchen. Soon Robin climbed to the top of the pantry and stretched out on a shelf not more than twelve inches from the ceiling. He hid there, unnoticed even when a servant opened the pantry door.

One by one, the servants finished their work and went off to bed. The room was quiet, and Robin wondered if it was safe to come down. Just then the pantry door opened again. "Robin!" It was Little John.

"I'm here," Robin said, and he unfolded himself from the narrow shelf and crawled slowly to the floor.

The giant stared at the floor. "Robin, I'd like to come back to you," he said.

"But why did you come here?" Robin asked.

"I thought I could help you! I thought I could find out something about the Sheriff that maybe you didn't already know!"

"And what have you found out?"

"Well, nothing, really." Little John whispered.

Robin touched his bulky forearm. "You have not betrayed us?"

Little John looked up, startled. "Betrayed you? Never, Robin! I owe my life to you!"

"Alright, alright." Robin smiled. "Of course you can come back. I've been worried about you."

Robin offered his hand, but instead Little John smothered him in a hug. "Go back to the courtyard," Little John told him. "Several of the merchants have fallen asleep there, the lousy drunks! Early tomorrow we'll make our move!"

Robin found the scene as Little John had described it. Snoring hulks occupied every corner of the courtyard. Robin curled up beside one group of three, making a pillow of the largest man's shoulder.

In the quiet darkness before sunrise, Little John tried to rouse Robin. "Are you coming with me?" he whispered as Robin wiped his face with one hand and scratched his head with the other. Robin wanted to get word to Fitz-water—and to Marian—that all had turned out well. "I'm coming, but not yet," he said. "You go on without me," he told Little John. "Go first to Will-o-the-Green. Then go to Warrenton and tell him to have the men prepare a feast." Robin was talking faster now, as his idea took shape. "Make it the finest feast we can serve," he said. "Tell them I'm bringing an important guest."

"But who are you bringing, Master Robin?"

"The Sheriff of Nottingham himself!"

"How will you do that?"

"Leave that to me. Now, go! Hurry up." The giant could move quietly when he needed to, and this morning he slipped out of the courtyard without so much as kicking a pebble. Robin tiptoed through another entrance, past a sleeping guard, and raced through back streets to the leaf-carved door of Neville Fitzwater.

He knocked three times, one time, and three times again. Just as before, the pinch-faced servant opened the door, and they repeated the password. Just as before, she led him through the kitchen to the hallway by the stairs. But Fitzwater was still asleep. The servant awakened him, and Robin hurriedly told his story.

"Stay here till tonight, and I'll help you safely out of the city," said Fitzwater.

"No, I must get back. I have a plan. Don't worry. I'll be careful." He shook the man's hand. "And I will be back, sir, you can be sure of that."

"Robin!" It was Marian, her hair unbound and flowing freely over her shoulders and down her back. She wore a cotton gown as white as newfallen snow.

"Marian," Fitzwater said. "Robin was just leaving. Will you show him to the door?"

"Of course, Father." She ushered Robin back through the kitchen. "When will I see you again?" she asked him.

"Very soon I hope," he said. He held her hands and tried to take in every detail of her beautiful face. "I— I love you, Marian."

"I know," she said with a small smile. "And I love you too, Robin Hood!"

He kissed her and then looked out on the alley to make sure no one would see him leave. "Wait for me," he whispered to her, and then he ran back toward the Sheriff's castle.

CHAPTER 18

The Set-Up

Robin raced through back streets till he got within sight of the Sheriff's castle. Then he forced himself to act his part once again. He slowed to a shuffling step and smiled with a silly grin. He sang nonsense rhymes as he ambled down the road.

When he got inside the castle, he found the courtyard in an uproar. Each minute, it seemed, one of the Sheriff's men-at-arms hauled in a villager, till there were more than twenty men standing between two guards along one wall.

Soon the Sheriff himself appeared. In a moment Robin realized why these men had been gathered in the courtyard. The Sheriff was

209

looking for Little John! The Sheriff cross-examined the men as his daughter strutted in front of them, shoving her bony nose in their faces, and wailing about what had happened. Her loud talk let Robin know what was going on.

Something had been stolen—the Sheriff's prized plate made of solid gold, and a sterling silver pitcher. Little John had said nothing about that to Robin. But Little John was the prime suspect in the crime, in Robin's mind as well as the Sheriff's. None of the men in this line, however, was as tall as Little John, as big as Little John, or as strong as Little John. And after more than thirty minutes of questioning, arguing, and babbling, the Sheriff and his impossible daughter decided that none of these men *was* Little John.

Robin edged closer to the group, being careful to keep his face out of the Sheriff's view. He had a plan for luring the Sheriff to the forest, but he would need to get near him if his plan was to work. Soon his chance came.

"You're all dismissed," the Sheriff said with a grand gesture to the frightened men.

"But, Daddy!" his daughter whined, as the men hurried away. "We must get the golden plate back! You know how I *loved* that golden plate—I could see myself in it! That stupid old silver pitcher was ugly, but we *can't* let that plate get away!" She folded her arms and pouted like a three-year-old.

"You're right, of course, my little melon blossom." The Sheriff patted her on both shoulders. "We shall get to the bottom of this, I promise you!" He turned to one of the guards. "Charles, we must continue the investigation! Now, tell me, who else might have taken my treasure?"

The man looked confused and afraid. And then his face brightened. "The merchants!" His eyes grew big with the idea. "Of course! The courtyard was full of merchants! Any one of those no-good, sticky-fingered food sellers could have taken your beautiful plate!" Just then the guard's eyes fell on Robin, hunched in a corner about six feet away. "You, there!" he hollered. "You were here last night! Grab him. Grab him!"

Two more of the Sheriff's guards seized Robin and tossed him against the wall where the other villagers had stood. "Round up all the merchants!" the Sheriff ordered. "We'll find the thief before the day is done!"

Soon another line of suspects had been formed. Robin was in the middle, entertaining them with his silly statements and nonsense.

"I've got me a farm, I have!" he sputtered. "And it's full of cattle, that's for sure!"

"Oh really, is that so?" said a pot-bellied farmer beside him. "And what kind of cattle do you have on this farm, you fool?"

"B-i-g ones!" said Robin, spreading his arms wide. The men around him laughed.

"Hey, there, what's this merriment while I make an official investigation?" The Sheriff marched over to the scene in a huff.

Robin kept talking. "Yeah, b-i-g cows, and I'm gonna sell 'em." The men looked with

amazement as Robin seemed unfazed by the Sheriff's presence. "I *am* gonna sell 'em!" he insisted. Robin grabbed one of the merchants by his collar. "I sold some of 'em yesterday, I did! For *twenty* pieces each. And I've got five *hundred* more at home. I'm gonna be *rich!*"

The Sheriff looked more curious than angry. "I say, young fellow," he began, "I would be interested in buying your cattle."

"You would?" Robin let out a deep-throated giggle.

"Yes! Of course!" The Sheriff smiled. "And I'll give you twice what you're asking!"

"Oh, my lord. Oh, my lord," Robin repeated over and over again, bowing before the Sheriff. "You won't be sorry. You won't be sorry." He stood up and began babbling to the men around him. "He's gonna buy my cows. He's gonna buy my cows!"

"Daddy!" The Sheriff's daughter pouted again.

"Oh, be quiet, woman!" he muttered under his breath. "I'll sell these cattle for *twice* what

I pay for them! With the profit I can buy you *two* gold plates!" The Sheriff turned to Robin. "Very fine, then," he said. "Just drive your cattle into the market place, and you shall have your money!"

"Oh, no, sir, I couldn't do that. I could *never* do that! There's too many. I don't know how! They're close, sir." He grabbed the Sheriff's wrist. "Come see 'em for yourself. Come pick your own cows!"

The Sheriff shook himself free from Robin's waving hand. "You stay here," he said to him. "Let these men go!" he ordered the guards. "The thief is clearly not in this bunch."

The happy merchants rushed out of the courtyard.

"Daddy, why would you trust this man?" The Sheriff's daughter hung on his shoulder.

"Woman! Have you no business sense at all? Can't you see that *someone* will make a *fortune* off this simpleton. It might as well be *me!*"

CHAPTER 19

The Captive

It was almost noon by the time the Sheriff and Robin had set off for the forest. The Sheriff's big seat spilled over his saddle. His flabby hips shook with each step his struggling pony took. Driving the butcher's cart, Robin whistled, or sang his silly rhymes, or jabbered nonsense.

They were close to Gamewell when Robin heard a familiar voice ahead of them. A man was singing a chant, a chant that Robin had heard before in the little chapel at Copmanhurst. The Friar was walking down the road toward them!

"Aye, there, Father," Robin called.

"Hello, my sons," the priest nodded. "God has given us a beautiful day in the forest, eh?"

The priest blocked the road, and Robin and the Sheriff had no choice but to rein their horses and stop.

"What do you want, Father?" the Sheriff said, just managing to hide his irritation with this interruption.

"Well, gentlemen, I was wondering if you could answer a question for me?"

The Sheriff sighed with frustration. "Out with it, man! What do you want?"

"Please tell me, sir," he said to the Sheriff, but he winked at Robin. "Do the deer run wild in the forest?"

Robin shouted the answer: "Only as long as the King allows!" He heard a shrill bugle in the woods beside them, and in an instant they were surrounded by twelve of his men, headed by Will Stutely!

The Sheriff snapped his horse's reins, and galloped toward Nottingham. The charging animal knocked both Midge and Middle out of the way. But the rest of Robin's men were ready with their bows, and at once a shower of arrows surrounded the Sheriff.

He pulled his horse off the path, dismounted, and hid behind a tree. "Don't kill me!" he whimpered as he peered around the trunk. "Here, I'll give you my horse. I'll give you a gold penny. Just *please,* don't hurt me!"

"But, sir, we do not intend to hurt you!" Robin threw aside the butcher's apron, let down his hood, and put on his forester's hat. "We want to invite you to a meal!" he said triumphantly, as the rest of the men gathered around him and the frightened Sheriff.

"You are ... Robin of Locksley!" the Sheriff gasped as Will Stutely and John Berry grabbed him by either arm.

"That is what you have called me," Robin answered as he jumped onto a tree stump. "But I am a different man, now. And so I will take a different name! It is a name given me by my own true love, and I shall wear it from this time forward. You, dear Sheriff," he said, with an overdone bow to the man, "and all of you too," he added as he gestured to the foresters around him, "shall call me Robin-o'-the-Hood—Robin Hood!"

The men were silent, as if they didn't know how to react.

"It is a foolish name," the Sheriff sneered.

"It is a fine name," Will Stutely finally said. "Welcome back to the greenwood, Robin Hood!" He shook Robin's hand, and the men cheered.

Robin tilted his head and let loose a deep belly laugh. "We must be on our way! We don't want to miss our special banquet!"

The men laughed and cheered again as they pushed the Sheriff back onto his horse and tied his hands to his saddle. John Berry blindfolded him and took the reins of his horse, guiding it along the path in the middle of the group.

It was almost evening when they arrived at Robin's camp. Will-o-the-Green's men were there too, and Will-o-the-Green ran to greet Robin and his group.

"I see you've brought a special guest!" Will said.

"A promise is a promise!" answered Robin. His arm across Will's shoulder, Robin walked with him to a bench across the camp and told him all the details of his adventure.

Meanwhile, Robin's men had dragged the Sheriff off his horse and removed his blindfold. He stumbled as his eyes adjusted to the sudden light, and they plopped him down at a banquet table where the men were beginning to gather.

Everyone was in high spirits. Not often did the men from both camps eat together. And never before had they enjoyed anything more than Robin's tale of hoodwinking the Sheriff and tricking him into the forest.

They ate wild venison, brown bread, and cooked apples. They jostled and punched the Sheriff who only stared glumly at his plate.

"Eat, your honor! We have spread this feast for you!" He ignored them.

"It's not polite to refuse your host's food!" He did not raise his head.

"Perhaps you would have a heartier appetite if you had a finer plate!" This time the Sheriff jerked his head to see who spoke to him. He looked up to see Little John's hulk hovering over him.

"You! You are the kitchen scum I was looking for!"

"And now you've found me," Little John answered. "Now, eat your dinner, and then you can tell us what you're going to do with me!" With this, Little John lowered to the Sheriff's place his own golden plate that Little John had stolen from his kitchen.

The Sheriff's eyes almost bugged out of his head. "I knew you took it. I knew it! You miserable, thieving low life! I ought to—"

"Perhaps a drink of ale will calm you," Little John said, and he poured a tankard full from the sterling silver pitcher he had also taken from the Sheriff's pantry.

"Oh!" the Sheriff shouted. He tried to stand, but the men on either side of him

grabbed his arms and pulled him back into his seat. The Sheriff fumed and muttered, and his bulging red cheeks made him look as if he were going to burst.

He was stuck there for more than thirty minutes while the men all around him enjoyed their meal with glee.

When most were done eating, Robin stood up again. "Now, Little John, it's time to give the Sheriff his bill for the meal he has enjoyed this evening!"

All at once the Sheriff's face turned white. "I did not bring my purse on the journey!" he said.

"Oh, really?" answered Robin. "And how were you going to pay me for my 'cattle'?"

"Well, of course, I did bring some cash with me, just a small sum."

"And what is that sum, my lord?" Little John said with mock respect.

"Certainly no more than forty pieces of gold."

"Wonderful!" Robin said. "I believe forty pieces of gold is the exact amount we were planning to charge! Isn't that right, Little John?"

"Yes, Master Robin," he agreed. He stood over the man, smiling, but flexing and unflexing his massive hands.

The Sheriff had no choice but to pay. "This is an outrage!" he growled as he reached for a leather pouch attached to his belt.

"Let me inspect your wallet, sir," Robin said.

"No, no, that's alright."

"Please sir," Robin said as Little John ripped the pouch off the Sheriff's belt and tossed it to him. "The woods are full of robbers, and so is your city of Nottingham. We must make sure no one has stolen your forty pieces of gold."

Robin held the pouch high in the air, opened it as everyone watched, and dumped onto the table in front of him a mound of coins worth at least twice what the Sheriff had admitted he brought.

"A bonus!" Robin shouted. "Payment for the food AND help for the poor villagers of Locksley!"

The men cheered and began chanting, "Bo-nus! Bo-nus!" They pounded the table in time with the chant, and soon they were on their feet, parading around the table.

The party continued into the night, with the Sheriff tied to a tree stump on one side of the camp. As the men laughed and talked and sang around a crackling fire, Robin sat to one side, watching it all.

Warrenton saw Robin sitting by himself and left his place by the fire to sit beside him. "Are you glad to be back, Master Robin?"

"Yes," Robin answered quickly. "But—" Robin broke a stick he had been using to stir the dirt.

"Robin, what is it?"

"Promise you won't laugh at me, Warrenton?"

"Of course." Warrenton stared at Robin, trying to see what was bothering him. Then, with a flash of understanding, he said, "It's the woman, isn't it?"

"She's more beautiful than I remembered," Robin told him. "I want to see her again— soon."

"Why not tomorrow?" Warrenton said. "We can't keep the Sheriff here forever. We'll dump him in the forest near Gamewell, and you can sneak back into Nottingham."

Robin smiled. "I can be in and out of the city before the Sheriff stumbles back."

Warrenton smiled. "It's a good plan."

CHAPTER 20

The King

Robin felt his heart beating in time with the clip-clop of the horses' hooves. He realized his plan was dangerous, but he didn't care. Just the thought of holding Marian's hand again was enough to make him risk anything.

Robin had brought only five men with him: Middle, Midge, John Berry, Will Stutely, and Warrenton. They were plenty to guard the exhausted Sheriff who even now nodded and dozed as he bounced on his pony.

They rode in silence through the chilly morning. Soon they came to a golden meadow bathed in sunlight.

"Be alert!" Robin reminded his men. It was the one place on the route that wasn't thick with trees. The little caravan would be out in the open for five minutes or more. If the Sheriff's men-at-arms had become suspicious and mounted a search party, this would be a perfect place for an ambush.

Robin raised his hand at the edge of the clearing, and the group halted. Each man peered across the meadow, looking and listening for anything suspicious.

"Let's go," said Robin, and the column entered the opening.

No sooner had they all left the cover of the trees than Robin stopped them again. "What's that?" he said.

They cocked their heads and listened carefully.

"Horses!" whispered John Berry. "Three of them, I think. Galloping through the woods ahead of us."

All six dismounted and crouched behind their horses. They left the Sheriff in front of them, tied to his horse.

They peered at the road on the other side of the meadow. Soon the first rider appeared. Robin could not tell who it was. Then two more men stopped their horses behind him. The first had gray hair the color of armor. The second was younger—he sported an un-trimmed black beard.

"Fitzwater!" gasped Robin. "And Geoffrey!"

Robin sprung from behind his horse and began running toward them. At once they recognized him and galloped to meet him in the middle of the clearing.

"Geoffrey!" said Robin. "They told us you were in France!"

"And that I was, but the turn of events brought me home."

"What events?"

"Robin," said Fitzwater. "King Henry is dead."

"And Prince John?"

"His rebellion has failed," said Geoffrey. "His brother Richard has become King!"

"And where does this leave you?" asked Robin, searching their faces for a clue to the future.

"It's all right, Robin," Fitzwater said calmly. "King Richard has vowed to make no difference between Norman and Saxon. He has dubbed Geoffrey Earl of Nottingham, and he's waiting in Nottingham now for an audience with the Sheriff." Fitzwater glanced at the Sheriff and then smiled at Robin. "I heard about your antics in the Sheriff's courtyard, and I figured that you had him. Geoffrey was showing me and my man to your camp."

They were close to Gamewell, but instead of leaving the Sheriff in the forest as they had planned, they kept him with them all the way to Nottingham.

He was pale and quiet. He seemed frightened to face the new King. But Robin was excited. Fitzwater and Geoffrey assured him that the new King was their friend. In fact, he had asked about Robin and wanted to meet him!

They found Nottingham in a festive mood. The market was full of buyers and sellers. People on the street seemed excited and happy. And a crowd had gathered outside the Sheriff's castle, waiting for the King to appear.

The heavy wooden drawbridge was down across the moat that surrounded the castle.

King's guards on chocolate-colored horses sat on either side of the bridge. They carried purple and scarlet banners. Gold-trimmed purple and scarlet silk blankets covered the horses' flanks.

The ten horsemen rode silently past the guards into the castle courtyard. A large crowd was inside, but they too became quiet when they saw Geoffrey, Fitzwater, the Sheriff, and the six foresters. King Richard himself sat on a wide, high-backed chair on a platform at the far side of the courtyard.

"Daddy!" the Sheriff's daughter gasped as she saw her father in the center of the group. She sat with John Ford between King's guards on one side of the courtyard.

The new King watched with piercing black eyes. Many called him Richard the Lion-Hearted. Robin did not know about his heart, but his head looked like a lion's. A mane of hair, auburn and white, flowed over his shoulders. And his beard, more white than auburn, reached below his neck.

Geoffrey and Fitzwater led them to his temporary throne, dismounted, and bowed before him. The others quickly followed their example.

"And so," the King said in a deep, strong voice, "has the Sheriff of Nottingham finally arrived home?"

"Y-yes, your Majesty." The Sheriff's voice was high and thin. "W-welcome to my home. I trust everything here is to your liking."

"No," the King responded. "Very much here is not to my liking! But if I had expected to be pleased by what I found here, I would not have visited so soon."

"B-but, your Majesty, whatever do you mean? I— We— Surely my servants have made you comfortable here?"

"I did not come to seek comfort," the King said in a louder voice. "I came seeking justice, but I have found none here."

"But, your Majesty—"

"Silence!" the King roared. "You have multiplied taxes on these poor people, so that you can live in luxury. You have thrown them into prison whenever you like, without trials and ignoring the laws. You have tortured and punished any who opposed you!"

The Sheriff lowered his head, and his hands trembled.

"But," the King continued, "You have been loyal to my father the King. And so I will not bind you in your own chains." The Sheriff

raised his head. "Instead I will leave you with my **strongest warning,**" the King said. "Geoffrey Montfichet is now Earl of Nottingham, and he will see to it that you obey my command. If I hear one word that you have gone back to your old ways, I will drag you to London and you will rot in my dungeon!"

"Yes, your Majesty." Two of the King's guards stepped forward and escorted the Sheriff to an empty chair beside his daughter.

The King turned his gaze to the others standing before him. "And which of you is Robin of Locksley?" he asked.

"I, sir." Robin stepped forward and knelt again.

"My father spoke to me of your father," Richard said. "He knew of his loyal service. And he knew that the Sheriff cheated you out of your rightful position after his death. He knew that your mother did not deserve the difficult life the Sheriff created for her."

"Thank you, your Majesty."

"And he also knew about your exploits in the forest," the King said. Robin felt a knot tying in the pit of his stomach. The King paused, stroking his beard, and looking carefully at the young man before him. "What do you have to say for yourself?" he asked.

Robin cleared his throat. "Your Majesty, you said you are looking for justice. Justice is what I have always sought. When the Sheriff chased me from my home, the forest became my home, and he became my enemy. We never robbed poor and struggling villagers. But we did touch the pockets of scoundrels like him so that we could help the poor."

"And now I want to make right the injustices of the Sheriff and others like him," the King said. "But we must have peace in the woods! Sherwood Forest must be safe for travelers."

Robin was silent as the King paused again. Then he pointed his finger straight at him. "Will you, Robin of Locksley, pledge to me your loyalty?"

240

"Yes, of course, your Majesty!"

"Then kneel before me." The King glanced at a guard who brought him a giant saber. "I dub you Earl of Huntingdon," the King proclaimed, as he touched the sword to each of Robin's shoulders.

Suddenly everyone in the courtyard broke into applause. Amazed, Robin kissed the King's hand, and then stood to face the cheering crowd.

In the wall of applauding people before him, he saw only one face. It was delicate, like a flower, framed with shiny black curls. Blue eyes sparkled, and a rose mouth smiled. Robin smiled too.

He had planned to sneak into Nottingham so he could see her again. But here as the Earl of Huntingdon, in the presence of the King, Robin was gazing at the woman he loved.

CHAPTER 21

The Celebration

It was the perfect day for a wedding. Warm sunshine streamed through the windows of the Nottingham church. Robin stood at the front, beside the altar, waiting for his bride to march down the aisle. Beside him stood his best man, Geoffrey Montfichet, Earl of Nottingham. Beside Geoffrey stood Will-o-the-Green, Will Stutely, and Warrenton, all of them decked out in their finest.

Robin smiled at his mother, who sat on the front row beside her brother, George Montfichet, the Squire of Gamewell. He thought of his father and wished he could be here. Would he ever have dreamed all that had happened? Could he ever have imagined Robin's days of hiding in the forest or his mother's difficult life while John Ford was trying to take over as Ranger of Locksley? Could he ever have foreseen the broken relationship between Robin and his uncle George Montfichet? And would he have ever believed that such a wound could be healed?

Robin looked now at his uncle and the old man smiled. He was happy with the new position his son had taken. They had reconciled. The man could die happy.

The music swelled, and Marian, on her father's arm, appeared at the back of the sanctuary. Robin's heart beat faster. Would his father have ever predicted that Robin would be marrying such a perfect jewel as Marian and that the King himself would be attending the ceremony?

Ahead of Marian and her father, two pink-dressed little girls spread flower petals down the aisle. As the bride entered, everyone stood and remained standing until Marian and her father had reached the front.

The Sheriff sat in the second row, beside his daughter. She was pale and grim-faced until Marian appeared. Then she began crying, softly at first. But by the time Marian and her father had reached the front, she was weeping uncontrollably. Her sobs filled the silence after the church's organ stopped playing the wedding march. After a few seconds, she stood up abruptly, crawled out of her pew, and stomped down the side aisle of the sanctuary.

But Robin and Marian didn't even hear her, didn't even notice, because their eyes were locked in each other's gaze.

The Friar performed the ceremony in his best Latin. When he pronounced them husband and wife, the organ played a majestic recessional, and the church bells rang throughout the city.

Outside, it seemed that everyone in the village had come to see the new couple and to cheer the King. The wedding party formed a grand parade through the town. Robin's men led the group, followed by the King, and then Robin and Marian. All of them rode perfect white horses from the King's own stables. Eleanor Fitzooth and George Montfichet rode at the back, in one of his carriages, followed by a dozen of the King's men-at-arms.

Each of Robin's men carried a burlap bag bulging with silver coins. As they paraded through Nottingham, they threw handfuls into the crowds. Robin had never heard such loud cheering. He had never felt such a spirit of celebration. He had never known that such good will and happiness could exist.

The procession rode to Gamewell where Montfichet's servants had prepared a magnificent banquet table. King Richard sat at the head, with the newlyweds beside him.

After the meal he stood and promised his subjects that peace would reign in the land. Then he conferred on George of Gamewell

full rank as Baron of the Realm, with power to speak and vote in the Upper Court of Appeal. It was the highest rank in the land, next to the King himself. Everyone cheered and toasted the new Baron.

Then the King turned to Marian. "I grant to you all the lands of Broadweald in Lancashire to hold as your own forever. Thus you shall have wealth to share with your Robin. Now use it wisely, be ready to serve me when I call, and live for God all your days." Then he raised her hands to his lips. "I wish you, fair lady, every joy that you could wish for yourself."

Marian beamed. Robin smiled. Montfichet patted Eleanor's hand. The crowd cheered. And the couple kissed. There was no reason to believe that the King's wish would not come true.